J. W. FERNANDEZ
14 MITCHELL LANE
HANOVER, N. H. 03755

THE THEORY OF SOCIAL STRUCTURE

By the same author

A BLACK BYZANTIUM
THE NUBA
THE FOUNDATIONS OF SOCIAL ANTHROPOLOGY
NUPE RELIGION

THE THEORY OF SOCIAL STRUCTURE

by

S. F. NADEL

LATE PROFESSOR OF ANTHROPOLOGY
IN THE AUSTRALIAN NATIONAL UNIVERSITY

WITH A MEMOIR BY
MEYER FORTES
WILLIAM WYSE PROFESSOR OF SOCIAL ANTHROPOLOGY
IN THE UNIVERSITY OF CAMBRIDGE

THE FREE PRESS
GLENCOE, ILLINOIS

COPYRIGHT
FIRST PUBLISHED 1957
PRINTED IN GREAT BRITAIN

PREFACE

THIS book is in essence the somewhat enlarged version of a series of lectures which I gave, with the same title, at the London School of Economics during the Lent Term of 1955. I am greatly indebted to the Director of the School, Sir Alexander Carr-Saunders, for having invited me to do so. My greatest debt is to Professor Raymond Firth, with whom the idea of the lectures (and of their subject) originated. I owe a further debt, for many helpful comments and criticisms, to him as well as to other friends: Miss Elizabeth Bott, Dr. Phyllis Kaberry, Dr. J. A. Barnes, Mr. M. Freedman, and Professor I. Schapera. They will, I think, find most of the points they raised reflected in this final version of the lectures. If this is not true of every point it is not for want of attention on my part but because I felt, rightly or wrongly, that I could do justice to the issues concerned in my own fashion.

S. F. N.

Canberra,
    January 1956.

CONTENTS

CHAPTER		PAGE
	Preface	v
	Memoir	ix
I	Preliminaries	1
II	Problems of Role Analysis	20
III	Conformity and Deviance	45
IV	The Coherence of Role Systems	63
V	Degrees of Abstraction	97
VI	Structure, Time and Reality	125
VII	Conclusions: Structure and Function	153

SIEGFRIED FREDERICK NADEL

1903-1956

A MEMOIR

PROFESSOR S. F. NADEL was one of the group of mature students who were appointed to Fellowships for field research in Africa by the Rockefeller Foundation and the International Institute of African Languages and Cultures in 1932. He came to the London School of Economics that year to work with C. G. Seligman and Bronislaw Malinowski in preparation for his field research. That was where we first met. We saw much of each other during that academic year, both in classes and at home, and we sailed in the same ship for our field research in West Africa in December 1933. That year of eager discussion, mutual criticism, and cheerful speculation among the group of young anthropologists at the L.S.E. had a decisive influence on all of them. And Nadel was in the centre of it. In class or out of it, an argument could not flag with him around.

What impressed everybody who met Nadel at that time was the fertility of his ideas and the unusual range of his knowledge and interests. What made him so stimulating was his boldness in putting forward his own ideas and his quick response to other points of view. He owed something of this to his background and education. When he came into anthropology he had already taken his doctorate in the University of Vienna in Psychology and Philosophy under two famous teachers, Karl Bühler and Moritz von Schlick. This training partly explains the command of contemporary psychological and philosophical theories displayed in his *Foundations of Social Anthropology* and the present book. But before that he had studied music, both from the performing and the academic side, and he had begun to make a name with his publications on the psychology and philosophy of music, in particular a book on musical typology. Just before coming to London he had been working on musicology with von Hornbostel and Kurt Sachs in Berlin studying the music of primitive peoples, and with Professor D. Westermann on African linguistics. But in between his academic pursuits he had produced programmes of exotic music for Radio Vienna, had toured Czechoslovakia with his own opera company, and had written a biography of F. B. Busoni. It needed exceptional gifts to achieve so much by the age of thirty, and Nadel had them. They were gifts not only of intellect and talent but of personality and of an outlook on life. Whatever he undertook was carried through speedily, indefatigably and thoroughly—and, above all, with that twist of individuality and enthusiasm that made it unmistakably his.

Nadel found an ideal outlet for his many-sided abilities in social anthropology. He was a first-rate linguist as his field work richly shows. Aided by his musical training, he learnt Hausa before going out to Nigeria and Nupe in the field. The great wealth of material in his Nuba book, considering the time and circumstances in which the field work was done, is due in no small measure to his flair for linguistic and, by extension, cultural nuances. Again, Nadel was by temperament and training drawn to theoretical problems and to the exciting but difficult borderland between anthropology and psychology. But he also had a strong practical and aesthetic bent, and he was as much at home among the commonplace and concrete (a favourite word of his) facts of routine ethnography as with abstract ideas. The solid detail in everything he published shows this. It was even more striking in his lectures and in discussion, when he moved back and forth between the facts of observation and his abstract analysis.

Nadel and his wife spent the year 1934 among the Nupe. I remember meeting him after we both got back from West Africa in 1935. He was agog with his experiences and excited about the unforeseen problems he had struck. He had found a political and legal order comparable to the nation state, bound up with a sophisticated economy and quite complex military and fiscal institutions, and based on a hierarchy of class and rank. It was, moreover, a culturally composite state with a documented history. Functionalist theory of the thirties could not deal adequately with this type of social system. It was a challenge and Nadel was delighted to have to work out his own solutions. He sketched these out in a paper published in 1935[1] and later expounded them fully in *A Black Byzantium*, published in 1942. Lord Lugard's preface to that book hints at, but hardly does justice to the great advance it represented in African sociology and in the theory of comparative politics.

Nadel and his wife returned to the Nupe in November 1935 for a second tour. This time Nadel broadened his scope to take in the psychological aspect of culture. While in England he had been invited by Professor F. C. (now Sir Frederic) Bartlett of Cambridge to take part in discussions with a group of psychologists and social scientists on the general problems of theory and method in social studies. The outcome was a book[2] to which Nadel contributed one article on the application of intelligence tests in anthropology and another on the interview technique. But he was not content only to weigh up what others had done. He decided to make his own experimental studies; and this is what he did in 1935, when he devised and applied a series of tests to several culturally different groups in Nigeria in order to examine the influence of culture on intellectual processes.

These experimental researches were by no means just a sideline. Later, in Australia, he returned to the problem. They were a means of exploring the question which is central to *The Foundations of Social Anthropology* and which also prompted Nadel to make a close and critical study of the work of the 'Culture and Personality' schools in anthropology. It was the question, on the theoretical plane, of how to unify the conceptual system of sociology and social anthropology with an appropriate psychological frame of analysis. In practical terms this pointed to the problem of how to link up orthodox field methods with some kind of experimental method.

Nadel was not long back from Nigeria when he was offered the appointment of Government Anthropologist in the Anglo-

[1] 'Nupe State and Community', *Africa*, VIII, 3, 1935.
[2] *The Study of Society: Methods and Problems*, Edited by F. C. Bartlett et al. 1939.

Egyptian Sudan, and from April 1938 to May 1939 he worked among the Nuba tribes. A short leave enabled him to finish *A Black Byzantium*; and then came the war.

The outbreak of war was a time of great trial for Nadel. He was an ardent and, indeed, impetuous person with a generally sanguine outlook. He poured his energies into his work and found his pleasure and relaxation in things of the mind and spirit. He was apt to think well, rather than ill, of his fellow man, in spite of the hard knocks he had had. For his was a generous nature. He was not particularly interested in politicians and their activities. But he had a very deep sense of duty as a citizen and as a man; and when it came to his moral and intellectual principles, he was uncompromising. Besides, he was an Austrian by birth and upbringing and he had lived and worked in Germany. He hated the Nazis and chafed to take an active part in the war against them.

But he had to wait for this. For he was recalled to his duties in the Sudan where he devoted the next two years to finishing his field work and producing his report on the Nuba tribes, later published under the title of *The Nuba* (1947). As soon as this was done he enlisted and was presently posted to military duties in Eritrea. From 1942 to 1945 he served in the British Military Administration in Eritrea, ending up with the rank of Major and the office of Secretary for Native Affairs. Commended by the Commander-in-Chief, M.E.F., 'for outstanding services', he was transferred in 1945, first to the Home Establishment and then to Tripolitania with the rank of Lieutenant-Colonel. There, too, he held the office of Secretary for Native Affairs in the British Military Administration and 'served with distinction, applying anthropology to the administration of peoples of various origin and tradition', as Sir Hubert Huddleston remarks in his Foreword to *The Nuba*. His army service ended in June 1946, when he was able, to his great joy, to come home for good to his wife and daughter.

Nadel now returned to academic anthropology. He had been appointed to a Senior Lectureship at the London School of Economics and took up his post in October 1946. He threw himself into teaching and writing with the urgency of one whose energies had for too long been pent up. Drawing on his wartime experience he wrote the papers on 'Land Tenure on the Eritrean Plateau'[1] which won him the Wellcome Medal of the Royal Anthropological Institute. He proved to be, as everyone expected, an inspiring teacher and efficient organiser. Thus when a Department of Anthropology was established in the University of Durham in 1948, he was the obvious choice as Reader and its first Head.

Two packed and fruitful years followed. *The Foundations of Social Anthropology* was finished, a remarkable feat even if it had not been accomplished at the same time as the creation of a new teaching department. There was a visit to the United States, where Nadel taught at Northwestern University during the summer of 1949 and made a notable impression. There was the usual run of academic committees and such like. Nadel, as I well remember, seemed to have unbounded vitality. And these two years were fittingly crowned by the award, in 1950, of one of the most prized honours in the world of anthropology, the Rivers Memorial Medal of the Royal Anthropological Institute, which is given for distinguished contributions to field research.

In 1950 a Chair of Anthropology and Sociology was created in the Research School of Pacific Studies, recently founded at the Australian National University, Canberra. Nadel was invited to be its first occupant. It was, again, an obvious choice. He had rapidly become one of the leading personalities in postwar British anthropology. It was taken for granted that Canberra would, with his leadership on its anthropological side, soon become a major centre of research in anthropological and social science. The prospect, I know, thrilled and excited him. There was a strong streak of adventurousness in Nadel and the idea of 'breaking new ground', in action as in his researches, had a great appeal to him. He saw a great opportunity for extending ethnographic fieldwork to new areas in the Pacific and, what interested him perhaps more, for putting some of his own and other people's theories to the kind of field tests he had in mind when writing the *Foundations of Social Anthropology*.

Nadel reached Australia early in 1951, having travelled via

[1] See *Africa*, XVI, Nos. 1 and 2, 1946.

the United States where he visited all the main university centres of anthropological teaching and research. With characteristic vigour, he was soon out in Papua and New Guinea planning his research programme, and before long he was sending young anthropologists recruited from Australia, this country, and the United States, out into the field. This was only the beginning of a wide range of activities, echoes of which came to his friends in England from time to time. In addition to running his research programme he took on the duties of Dean of the School of Pacific Studies. But administration—and Nadel was a very businesslike administrator—never stopped him from getting on with his own thinking and writing. Between 1951 and 1954 he brought out a series of papers which show him exploring further, and with no little daring, some of the hypotheses put forward in *The Foundations of Social Anthropology*, and turning his attention, as in his Inaugural Lecture in 1953, to the application of anthropology to problems of the modern world. His book on *Nupe Religion*, in which the theory of explanation expounded in *The Foundations* is put to the test of observation, came out in 1954. Yet he found the time and the energy to attend the International Symposium on Anthropology held under the auspices of the Wenner-Gren Foundation in New York in 1952, to take part in the Eighth Pacific Science Congress at Manila in 1953, and to make an extended tour in India under Unesco auspices in 1954, advising on research and giving lectures at several universities. A near-verbatim report of the discussions at the Wenner-Gren Symposium has been published[1] and this affords a unique record of Nadel's virtuosity in discussion.

In January 1955, to the great delight of his friends, Nadel, together with his wife and daughter, came to England on leave. He made his base at the London School of Economics but visited and lectured at Cambridge, Oxford and Manchester, and also attended a symposium on African customary law at Amsterdam. He even found time to record two talks on 'Magic Thinking' for the B.B.C. It was my privilege to introduce him to a large and representative audience when he gave a public lecture on Cargo Cults at Cambridge University. It was a

[1] *An Appraisal of Anthropology Today*, by Sol Tax et al.

masterly lecture delivered with effortless lucidity which won the admiration of the audience.

However, what Nadel was mainly occupied with during his leave was his writing and a course of lectures he was invited to give in his former department at the London School of Economics. These lectures formed the basis of the present book. It was completed for publication a week or two before his death. He had, at that date, in addition to this book, no less than six papers in the press, including his Presidential Address to Section F (Anthropology) of the Australian and New Zealand Association for the Advancement of Science, which held its Thirty-first meeting at Melbourne in August 1955. It is called 'Understanding Primitive Peoples' and as I read it a picture of Fred Nadel comes vividly to my mind's eye. Here he is engaged in a task he enjoyed and performed with characteristic good humour and skill, the task of explaining social anthropology to the non-specialist. Nadel believed strongly in the importance of explaining science to 'the man in the street' and he had the art of doing this for his own subject without giving the impression of talking down to the uninitiated. This was one reason why he was such an excellent broadcaster and public speaker. His Presidential Address is not, of course, directed to the public at large but to a general academic audience and Nadel does not hesitate to bring in matters of high theory, for example, when he refers to his concept of social signs.

What of the present book? This memoir is a tribute of regard and affection for a friend and professional comrade, not an Introduction to his last book. But I cannot end without a word about it. I am convinced that it is destined to be one of the great theoretical treatises of twentieth-century social anthropology. I doubt if any anthropologist of our generation other than Nadel would have had the courage to attempt it, or, indeed, the learning, the fertility of mind and the analytical acumen that have been called for in the undertaking. It puts the theory of social structure on a new plane.

This is not the place, nor is a friend and contemporary the right person to attempt to evaluate Nadel's total contribution to social anthropology. That must be left to a younger generation. It is enough to remind readers of the present book that his work has two sides. There is the ethnographical side represented by his field work monographs; these stand as a major contribution to our knowledge of African societies. And there is the more strictly theoretical side expressed in the present book and its predecessor, *The Foundations of Social Anthropology*. These, in my judgement, will have a lasting place in the fundamental literature of our subject.

Fred Nadel died suddenly, at the height of his powers and promise, on January 14th, 1956. It is a grievous loss to anthropology and an irreparable one to his friends. We must console ourselves with the thought of the splendid body of work he has bequeathed to us,[1] and, more especially, with our memories of the kind of man he was. Circumstances which would have embittered lesser men merely spurred him on to greater achievements; for he never bore a grudge, and generally looked on the hopeful side of things. Not that he lacked strong feelings. He could be a very angry man when confronted with anything mean or ignoble. He had a ready wit and his friends will remember many an evening enlivened by his genial conversation and wide knowledge. They will remember the warmth and immediacy of his friendship and the speed with which help and counsel came from him when they were wanted.

King's College,   MEYER FORTES
Cambridge
September 1956

---

[1] A complete bibliography will be published in the journal *Man*.

I

PRELIMINARIES

PERHAPS I should have called this book *Towards a Theory of Social Structure* or even *Thoughts on a Theory of Social Structure*, to indicate more faithfully its experimental nature. Also, much of it is of the clearing-the-decks type; and though this is a task both necessary and, I think, profitable, it cannot be claimed to produce a great deal in the way of final answers or definitive solutions.

Even the word 'theory' which appears in the title needs to be placed in the right perspective. Broadly speaking, we mean by a theory a body of interconnected propositions (hypotheses, generalizations) concerned with a particular problem area and meant to account for the empirical facts in it. Now in fully-fledged scientific theories 'accounting for' means 'explaining'. In this sense the interconnected propositions or generalizations are such that 'observable consequences logically follow'.[1] Differently put, they are such that the empirical facts within the range covered by the theory are deducible from it, so that their being what they are is predicted (by the theory) and understood (in the light of the theory). Needless to say, only the most advanced sciences have reached this level of explanatory theory-building. But 'theory' can also be understood in another, less ambitious, sense, namely as a body of propositions (still interconnected) which serve to *map out* the problem area and thus prepare the ground for its empirical investigation by appropriate methods. More precisely, the propositions serve to classify phenomena, to analyse them into relevant units or indicate their interconnections, and to define 'rules of procedures' and 'schemes of interpretation'.[2] 'Theory' here equals conceptual scheme or logical framework; and it is in this sense

[1] R. B. Braithwaite, *Scientific Explanation*, 1953, p. 22.
[2] Felix Kaufmann, *Methodology of the Social Sciences*, 1944, pp. 48, 161-2.

that the present enquiry can be said to aim at a 'Theory'. Actually, in one or two places I shall also advance what amount to explanatory hypotheses.[1] But they are presented incidentally, because the run of the argument leads in that direction, and not in any sense as crucial points in the 'theory'.

So much by way of introduction. Turning now to my proper subject I can do no better than take my lead from the statement, recently made by a prominent anthropologist, that 'notable advances have been made in the theory of social structure of homogeneous societies. . . . By comparison theories about culture are unsystematic and unco-ordinated.'[2] I do not wish to go into the latter assertion (which can, I think, easily be disproved). But I would suggest that, in anthropology, the very concept of social structure is still in a sense on trial. At least discussions about it still tend to be polemical (the passage just quoted being an example). This may seem surprising considering that in the sister-discipline, sociology, the concept gained wide currency almost from the start. The term appears already in the writings of Herbert Spencer and Durkheim,[3] and is rarely left unmentioned in modern literature. But there it is mostly used in a broad and almost blanket fashion, referring to any or all features contributing to the make-up of societies; it thus becomes simply a synonym for system, organization, complex, pattern, type, and indeed does not fall very short of 'society as a whole'. Take these examples: 'Social Structure is the web of interacting social forces from which have arisen the various modes of observing and thinking. . . .'[4] The study of 'social structure is concerned with the principal forms of social organization, i.e. types of groups, associations and institutions and the complex of these which constitute societies. . . . A full account of social structure would involve a review of the whole field of comparative institutions.'[5] 'Group structures' represent

[1] This is true, for example, of the principles of 'allocation' and 'dichotomization of roles' introduced later. (See pp. 35 et seq.).
[2] Meyer Fortes, *Social Anthropology at Cambridge since 1900*. (Inaugural Lecture, 1953, p. 39).
[3] Herbert Spencer, *Principles of Sociology*, 1885, vol. I, pp. 459 et seq.; *Social Statics*, 1892, p. 237; Emile Durkheim, *De la Division du Travail Social*, 1893, 6th ed., pp. 149 et seq.
[4] K. Mannheim, *Ideology and Utopia*, 1936, pp. 45-6.
[5] M. Ginsberg, *Reason and Unreason in Society*, 1947, pp. 1, 8.

the kind of reality 'into which we are born and within which we find work and recreation, rewards and penalties, struggle and mutual aid. . . .' All 'the various modes of grouping . . . together comprise the complex pattern of social structure. . . . In the analysis of the social structure the role of the diverse attitudes and interests of social beings is revealed.'[1]

In anthropology, on the other hand, the introduction of the term went together with the attempt to give it a narrower and precise definition. We owe both to Radcliffe-Brown,[2] whose students and followers have further developed and partly redefined the concept. But again, several anthropologists still prefer the broader, unspecific meaning of 'social structure', while others—especially in America—omit the term altogether, e.g. Linton in *The Study of Man* or Lowie in his *Social Organization*. One prominent anthropologist, Kroeber, explicitly questions its usefulness, stressing, perhaps a little intolerantly, the vagueness with which it tempts its users: ' "Structure" appears to be just yielding to a word that has a perfectly good meaning but suddenly becomes fashionably attractive for a decade or so —like "streamlining"—and during its vogue tends to be applied indiscriminately because of the pleasurable connotation of its sound.'[3]

If there are instances suggesting that the anthropologist can well do without an additional concept of so fluid a connotation, a case has also been made out for precisely this broader use. Thus Firth points out that 'any science must have a budget of terms of general application, not too closely defined, and . . . structure may be one of them'.[4] This is a weighty and persuasive argument; even so I shall, in the present discussion, take the opposite standpoint. I shall do so essentially heuristically, with a view to assessing the fruitfulness of the concept *if it be narrowly defined*. Nor is it difficult to defend this standpoint. It will hardly be denied that the addition of a new term to a technical vocabulary already well provided with rough equivalents cannot but suggest that it has a specific connotation, referring to a

---

[1] R. M. MacIver and C. H. Page, *Society*, 1950, pp. 209, 212.
[2] 'On Social Structure', *J.R.A.I.*, 1940, vol. 70, Part I.
[3] *Anthropology*, 1948, p. 325.
[4] *Elements of Social Organization*, 1951, p. 29.

range of problems or to methods of enquiry not previously isolated or perceived. In the case of a word like 'structure', which has a well-defined meaning in other disciplines, this seems doubly true. And ideally, considering scientific economy and consistency, the acceptance of any new terms might well be made subject to these conditions. Let us therefore apply these conditions and treat 'social structure' in this sense, as a novel and specialized conceptual tool the fruitfulness of which it is worth exploring.

Equally, this task of exploration is neither unwarranted nor redundant. For even among the scholars who present us with a clear-cut definition of social structure, there is little agreement, at least on the level of verbal formulation. All the students of social structure are agreed that in studying 'structure' we study essentially the interrelation or arrangement of 'parts' in some total entity or 'whole'. They are agreed, further, that the adjective 'social' specifies the character of that 'whole'—which is 'society' or any of its subdivisions, and not 'culture' and any of its sectors or provinces: which distinction is by now too well established to need further comment. We might only add that one or two scholars also employ the concept of structure in the latter sense. Thus Herskovits means by 'structure of culture', somewhat naively, the progressive combination of 'traits', in complexes, areas and patterns.[1] Bateson applies the same phrase, on a much more sophisticated level, to the 'logical' order (in terms of 'premises' or 'underlying assumptions') discernible in the modes of behaviour typical of a people.[2] More recently, Feibleman has advanced a similar view, equating the 'structure of culture' with the 'common axiom sets' from which 'all manifestations of a culture can be deduced.'[3]

Now as regards the concept of structure applied to 'society', though there is no dispute about the total entity whose division into parts is taken as the subject matter of structural studies, on the nature of the parts themselves views differ widely. Indeed, the variety of views gives rise to considerable confusion. Let us look at some of them.

[1] Melville J. Herskovits, *Man and his Works*, 1948, p. 169.
[2] Gregory Bateson, *Naven*, 1936, pp. 218-20.
[3] James K. Feibleman, 'Towards an Analysis of the Basic Value System' (*American Anthropologist*, vol. 56, 1954, p. 424).

Radcliffe-Brown in one of his more recent contributions, explains that 'the components of social structure are human beings', the structure itself being an 'arrangement of persons in relationships institutionally defined and regulated'.[1] There is a more recent definition still, which is interesting because its circularity betrays the difficulties inherent in the conceptualization of social structure: this is now said to be made up of 'human beings considered not as organisms but as occupying positions in social structure'.[2] Eggan finds the components or units of social structure in the inter-personal relations, which 'become part of the social structure in the form of status positions' occupied by individuals.[3] Evans-Pritchard restricts social structure to the interrelations of groups, explicitly excluding inter-personal relations.[4] Fortes once more accepts the latter as 'elements' of social structure, adding that they are reached through abstracting 'the *constant* features in the pattern of organization of all activities in which (the relation) is significant'.[5] But he also maintains that social structure contains 'parts and relations of diverse nature and variability' and pertains to 'social events and organizations' as their *'variable'* aspect.[6] For Leach, social structure (in so far as 'practical situations' are concerned) 'consists of a set of ideas about the distribution of power between persons or groups of persons'.[7] Finally, the latest edition of *Notes and Queries on Anthropology* advances the all-too-catholic definition of social structure as the 'whole network of social relations in which are involved the members of a given community at a particular time'; while Lévi-Strauss *per contram* holds that social structure 'can by no means be reduced to the ensemble of social relations to be described in a given society'.[8]

[1] In *African Systems of Kinship and Marriage*, ed. Daryll Forde and A. R. Radcliffe-Brown, 1950, p. 82.
[2] A. R. Radcliffe-Brown, *Structure and Function in Primitive Society*, 1952, pp. 9-10.
[3] *Social Organization of the Western Pueblos*, 1950, p. 5.
[4] *The Nuer*, 1940, p. 262.
[5] *The Web of Kinship Among the Tallensi*, 1949, p. 340.
[6] 'Time and Social Structure', in *Social Structure; Studies presented to A. R. Radcliffe-Brown*, 1949, pp. 56-7.
[7] *Political Systems of Highland Burma*, 1954, p. 4.
[8] 'Social Structure', in *Anthropology Today*, ed. A. L. Kroeber, 1953, p. 525.

It will be agreed, I think, that there is little to be gained from trying to reconcile these various conceptions. Let me, therefore, begin at the beginning and examine afresh the meaning which can usefully and logically be assigned to 'social structure'. I propose to proceed strictly operationally, that is, I shall attempt to specify, at every stage, the 'operations', observational or cognitive, which underlie any term used; and I hope that this procedure will not be regarded as unduly painstaking and circuitous or, for that matter, as belabouring the obvious.

I shall on occasion also employ a system of notation which I am attempting to develop, mainly on the basis of familiar symbols borrowed from mathematics and symbolic logic. I shall do so not in order to give a more 'scientific' appearance to my exposition, but because I firmly believe that social analysis in its present stage can profitably make use of such forms of notation, and is ready for them. Their purpose, to begin with at any rate, would be to help in demonstrating certain complicated situations more simply and accurately than can be done by verbose descriptions. This is obviously only a beginning, though I hope a promising one. And no part of social analysis seems more appropriate for making a start than the analysis of social structure which, as we shall presently see, is focused upon formal features and relations, that is, upon the kind of phenomena with which mathematics and logic pre-eminently deal.

Perhaps there is more to be said in defence of this new departure. It has been argued that sociological exposition and interpretation cannot help being 'highly discursive'; for 'sociology has few formulæ, in the sense of highly abbreviated symbolic expressions of relationships between sociological variables'.[1] If so, a system of symbolic expressions, even in the form of a mere notational system, must help towards a sharper and more concise manner of exposition. To be sure, the technique of notation will not by itself produce significant 'formulæ'; it does not automatically procure a fuller insight into the 'relationships between sociological variables'.[1] It only equips us with a new tool for demonstrating them, if or when they are discovered. But let us not minimize the usefulness of this equipment. New

[1] Robert K. Merton, *Social Theory and Social Structure*, 1949, p. 13.

tools have been known to facilitate new discoveries. They certainly produce, in those who use them, a new attitude, a new way of looking at the material to be handled: which is probably the decisive step.

2

We begin with the most general definition of 'structure', which underlies the use of the term in all other disciplines. There structure is a property of empirical data—of objects, events or series of events—something they exhibit or prove to possess on observation or analysis; and the data are said to exhibit structure inasmuch as they exhibit a definable articulation, an ordered arrangement of parts. Indicating articulation or arrangement, that is, formal characteristics, structure may be contrasted with *function* (meaning by this term, briefly, adequacy in regard to some stipulated effectiveness) and with *content, material* or *qualitative character*. The former contrast is too familiar to need illustration; the latter has a wide application in psychology, linguistics, and logic.

It should be noted in passing that in two instances at least 'social structure' is explicitly denied to have the character here envisaged, that is, to be a feature of 'empirical reality'. This view, expressed by Lévi-Strauss and Leach, will be discussed later (see p. 149). For the sake of completeness, we should add a third dichotomy to the two mentioned, i.e. *structure* and *process;* but this point, too, may at this stage be disregarded.

While the separation of structure from function implies a divergence of viewpoint and interest, the separation of structure from content, material, and qualitative character implies a move to a higher level of abstraction. For when describing structure we abstract relational features from the totality of the perceived data, ignoring all that is not 'order' or 'arrangement'; in brief, we define the positions relative to one another of the component parts. Thus I can describe the structure of a tetrahedron without mentioning whether it is a crystal, a wooden block, or a soup cube; I can describe the arrangement of a fugue or sonata without making any musical noises myself; and I can describe a syntactic order without referring to the phonetic material or semantic content of the words so ordered.

This has an important consequence, namely that structures can be transposed irrespective of the concrete data manifesting it; differently expressed, the parts composing any structure can vary widely in their concrete character without changing the identity of the structure. Our definition should thus be rephrased as follows: structure indicates an ordered arrangement of parts, which can be treated as transposable, being relatively invariant, while the parts themselves are variable. This definition, incidentally, fully corresponds to the one logicians would apply in their field: there too one speaks of an 'identical structure' in the case of any 'abstract set' which 'may have more than one concrete representation', the latter being potentially 'extremely unlike in material content'.[1]

Now to translate all this into the language appropriate to the analysis of societies. There is an immediate difficulty; for it is by no means easy to say precisely what a 'society' is.[2] But whatever we may wish to include in a sophisticated definition of society, certain things are clear and can be stated quite simply. To begin with, societies are made up of people; societies have boundaries, people either belonging to them or not; and people belong to a society in virtue of rules under which they stand and which impose on them regular, determinate ways of acting towards and in regard to one another. Conceivably, in theory, there might be as many such ways of acting as there are situations in which people meet, practically an infinite number. But we are here speaking of ways of acting governed by rules and hence in some measure stereotyped (or rendered 'determinate'). And of the ways of acting so understood it is true to say that they are finite and always less numerous than the possible combinations of people: which means that the same ways of acting are repetitive in the population. We need only add that these ways of acting are repetitive also in the sense that they apply to changing or successive populations.

Let me expand this a little. For 'determinate ways of acting towards or in regard to one another' we usually say 'relation-

[1] M. Cohen and E. Nagel, *An Introduction to Logic and Scientific Method*, 1947, p. 29.

[2] See my *Foundations*, pp. 183-5; Marion J. Levy, *The Structure of Society*, 1952, Chap. III; A. R. Radcliffe-Brown, *Structure and Function in Primitive Society*, 1952, p. 193.

ships', and we indicate that they follow from rules by calling them 'institutionalized' or 'social' (as against 'private' or 'personal') relationships. We identify the mutual ways of acting of individuals as 'relationships' only when the former exhibit some consistency and constancy, since without these attributes they would merely be single or disjointed acts. But what is constant or consistent is not really the concrete behaviour, with its specific quality or content. If it were so, the individuals involved in any relationship would have to act *vis-à-vis* one another always in precisely the same manner. Now we may disregard that inevitable variability which comes into play when actions, even though intended to be identical, are repeated on different occasions and in varying circumstances. There remain a few approximations to the kind of relationship which would produce the same uniform behaviour throughout. They are exemplified in relationships which are strictly utilitarian and revolve upon a single purpose, such as the relationship between fellow workers, between shopkeeper and customer, perhaps between teacher and pupil.

Most relationships, however, lack this simple constancy or uniformity. Rather, the *concrete* behaviour occurring in them will always be diversified and more or less widely variable, intentionally changing with the circumstances; it will be constant or consistent only in its *general character*, that is, in its capacity to indicate a certain type of mutuality or linkage. We may still say of persons in a given relationship that they act towards each other 'always in the same manner'; but 'manner' should be in the plural, and 'the same' understood very broadly. It is in virtue of this general character or broad 'sameness' that we regard a whole series of genuinely varying ways of acting as adding up to a single ('constant', 'consistent') relationship. Conversely, any relationship thus identified (and, incidentally, named as aptly as is possible) is understood to signify such a whole series subsumed in it.

Thus we take 'friendship' to be evidenced by a variety of mutual ways of acting, perhaps visible on different occasions, such as help in economic or other crises, mutual advice on various matters, efforts to be together, certain emotional responses. A 'respect relationship' will imply manners of greeting, a particular choice of language, advice sought and given, services offered and expected, etc. The parent-child relationship similarly includes actions exacting respect, behaviour indicative of love and care, and acts of a disciplinary or punitive kind. To say it again, the large majority of social relationships are of this inclusive and serial type (which Gluckman calls 'multiplex').[1] Differently expressed, each relationship has a whole range of 'concrete representations', implying them all. Thus, in identifying any relationship we already *abstract* from the qualitatively varying modes of behaviour an invariant relational aspect—the linkage between people they signify.

This can be shown symbolically by indicating the diverse *modes* of behaviour by small letters (a to n), the *condition* 'towards' or 'acting towards' by the sign':', and the implicitness of the modes of behaviour in the relationship by the logical sign for *implication*, '$\supset$'; we further indicate the fact that a relationship rests not on a single 'way of acting' but on a whole range or series by the mathematical symbol for 'series', Σ. Thus, when we say of any two persons A and B that they stand in a particular relationship r which, for the sake of simplicity, we will assume to be a strictly symmetrical one, we mean that

(1) $\quad$ A r B, if
$\quad\quad$ A (a, b, c ... n): B, and *vice versa;*
$\therefore r \supset \Sigma$ a ... n.

Firth holds very similar views on the process whereby we identify social relationships, or 'infer' them from some observed sequence of acts: 'We see sufficient elements of likeness to allow us to attribute identity, to abstract and generalize into a type of social relation'.[2] Let us note, however, that this abstraction and generalization does not go very far. We still need to distinguish relationships or types of relationships qualitatively, by their content of aims, emotions, etc. It is thus that we speak of friendship as against love or loyalty, separate respect from reverence or servitude, or distinguish between relationships having an economic, political, religious or perhaps purely emotive significance.

It is clear, on the other hand, that all relationships, through

[1] Max Gluckman, *The Judicial Process among the Barotse of Northern Rhodesia*, 1954, p. 19.
[2] Raymond Firth, *Elements of Social Organization*, p. 21.

the linkage or mutuality they signify, serve to 'position', 'order' or 'arrange' the human material of societies. And considering what we said before about the repetitiveness of relationships in the population, it follows that they do satisfy the criterion of invariance implicit in the concept of structure. They do so in the sense that every relationship has its several 'concrete representations' also in the widely varying individuals who may, at any time, be linked or positioned in the stated fashion.

But relationships are not irregularly repetitive, and the individuals acting in them not variable at random. (We may ignore relationships occurring fortuitously, for example, owing to sympathies or antipathies which happen to affect people: they do not concern us to any great extent since social enquiry is *ex hypothesi* about regularities, not accidents.) Rather, the recurrence of relationships is once more circumscribed by rules, the same set of rules which determines the 'ways of acting' of people towards one another. It is part of these rules that they also specify the type of individuals—any individual satisfying certain conditions or placed in certain circumstances—who can or must act in particular relationships. Expressed more simply, individuals become actors in relationships in virtue of some brief; which brief is obviously as invariant as the relationships that hinge on it. And instead of speaking of individuals 'being actors in virtue of some brief', we usually speak of individuals enacting *roles*.

This will become clearer a little later. At the moment only one further thing needs saying. Though relationships and roles (more precisely, relationships in virtue of roles) 'arrange' and 'order' the human beings who make up the society, the collection of existing relationships must itself be an orderly one; at least, it must be so if the ordered arrangement of human beings is indeed a total arrangement, running through the whole society. Think of a piece of polyphonic music: any two tones in it are positioned relative to one another by the intervals they describe; but the total design or structure of the piece clearly lies not in the mere presence and collection of all these intervals but in the order in which they appear. Though this analogy has drawbacks, it illustrates the point I wish to make if for intervals we read relationships and for musical structure, social structure.

Oddly enough, this question has rarely been raised, as a question. Most writers on social structure seem content to indicate that it is composed, in some unspecified manner, of persons standing in relationships or of the sum-total of these. Only Lévi-Strauss goes further, insisting that the mere 'ensemble' of existing relationships does not yet amount to 'structure' (see above, p. 5). Like myself, he thus stipulates a further 'order', over and above the one implicit in the relationships, and interrelating the latter. Let us note that this is not merely a two-level hierarchy of, say, first-order relations (linking and arranging persons) and second-order relations (doing the same with relationships). We are dealing here with differences in kind; the orderliness *of* a plurality of relationships differs radically from the ordering of a plurality of individuals *through* relationship. And whatever the precise nature of the former, we can see that it must correspond to something like an overall system, network or pattern.

We may break off at this point. We now have all the terms needed for a definition of social structure, and we may put it this way: We arrive at the structure of a society through abstracting from the concrete population and its behaviour the pattern or network (or 'system') of relationships obtaining 'between actors in their capacity of playing roles relative to one another'.[1]

Though this and similar definitions are basically correct (and must be so if our reasoning has been correct) they conceal serious methodological difficulties; for a satisfactory theory of social structure on this basis presupposes an adequate theory of roles, and none has yet been advanced in any systematic fashion. As a next step, therefore, I propose to make this attempt. But a few comments are still needed to complete this preliminary discourse.

3

(i) First, let me stress that the phrase 'playing roles relative to one another' in our definition of social structure does not merely mean 'playing roles *vis-à-vis* one another'; that is, we are not restricting social structure to face-to-face relationships or situations. This viewpoint hardly needs justifying. I mention it

[1] Talcott Parsons, *Essays in Sociological Theory*, 1949, p. 34.

only because in using the conventional phraseology (or one not too clumsy) one is apt to give the impression of considering primarily face-to-face situations. Relationships other than face-to-face do pose certain special technical problems such as appropriate machineries of communication. But the reliance, on the part of the society, on face-to-face relationships equally involves technical difficulties, now concerning facilities for the necessary physical propinquity of the actors. I shall disregard both questions, which refer to the prerequisite conditions of social structures rather than to social structure as such.

(ii) It might seem that the approach here proposed, starting from the concepts of roles and role-playing actors, must miss a whole province or aspect of social structure, namely that formed by the ordered arrangements of sub-groups and similar subdivisions of society. We may take it for granted that any society does contain within it a number of smaller and simpler replicas of itself, which we conventionally call sections, segments, sub-groups etc. Their presence and arrangement clearly represents as much an 'articulation' as does the division of society into role-playing actors. Which seems to suggest that our definition of social structure is incomplete and that, in order to make it complete, we have to mention not only relationships between actors or persons but also the interrelations between sub-groups. But this juxtaposition is deceptive in spite of the near-coincidence of the terms 'relationship' and 'interrelation'. The latter (applied to groups) is not a counterpart or parallel of the former (applied to persons), as even a cursory glance will show; for while the relationship of persons implies interaction between them, behaviour of one towards or in regard to the other, groups of which we say that they are inter-related do not interact or behave as such, collectively, save in relatively few, special cases. Rather we must look at the situation in a different way.

Sub-groups, like that widest group the 'society at large', are made up of people in determinate, stable relationships. And any group is characterized by the kinds of relationships that occur between the people in question, holding them together. Now inasmuch as sub-groups are discrete entities, bounded units, at least certain of these characteristic relationships must be equally bounded, that is, they must come to an end somewhere, their cessation demarcating the boundaries of the group. From this point of view, then, we might describe sub-groups as areas of bounded relationships. But inasmuch as they are also sub-divisions of a wider collectivity and not isolated, self-sufficient units, the bounded relationships must themselves be inter-related. In other words, they must exhibit or fit into the overall network or pattern we spoke of before. The interrelation of sub-groups is therefore only a special case of the relatedness or 'orderliness' of relationships, and our definition of social structure both covers it and will logically lead us to it.

For the sake of completeness I ought to add this further remark, if only in parenthesis. In a somewhat different frame of reference the bounded unity of groups (and of society at large) can be demonstrated more simply by the criterion of *co-activity*, i.e. by indicating the particular co-ordinated activity (or activities) which would hold between all persons in the human aggregate claimed to constitute a group. This is the criterion I in fact adopted in a previous study.[1] But though satisfactory in that context, the criterion is less so in the present one. For it is clear that a single embracing co-activity cannot always be translated into a single, equally embracing, relationship. This is feasible only if either the co-activity involves no differentiation in the position of the participants (so that ArB equals BrC . . . *ad inf.*), or the relationship considered is of a highly general kind (e.g. the 'fellowship' of fellow tribesmen or citizens, the 'kinship' of a group based on descent). But usually the former condition will be inapplicable or the latter too uninformative, and the embracing co-activity will need to be broken up into a series of distinct relationships in accordance with the different parts played by the participants. Thus, from the present viewpoint, directed as it is upon relationships, the more devious definition of group unity quoted above proves the only possible one.

(iii) I must now explain that the two terms, 'network' and 'pattern', are not meant as synonyms. Rather, they are intended to indicate two different types or perhaps levels of overall

[1] *The Foundations of Social Anthropology*, 1951, p. 186.

structuring with which we shall meet throughout this discussion but for which, frankly, I have not been able to find very satisfactory terms. The best way I can describe them is by saying that one type of structuring is abstracted from *interactions*, the other from *distributions*. The latter may in turn apply to a variety of things—to concrete populations, to persons in their roles, as well as to relationships and sub-groups. The terms 'network' and 'pattern' are meant to indicate this distinction primarily in regard to relationships.

Thus I shall mean by 'pattern' any orderly distribution of relationships exclusively on the grounds of their similarity and dissimilarity. It is best exemplified (there are other, less clearcut examples) by societies of the type Durkheim calls 'segmental', i.e. societies characterized by the 'repetition of like aggregates in them', the 'aggregates' being, for instance, clans, lineages, age sets or social strata.[1] Let me explain this more fully. Since any group or sub-group consists of an area of bounded relationships it follows that, if the sub-groups are repetitive, the relationships characterizing them will be distributed in a similarly repetitive manner. That is to say, the relationships will occur within each of the like units (or 'aggregates') but not outside or between them, disappearing or being replaced by different relationships at the group boundaries. Think of the particular fellowship linking age mates and age mates only; of the economic and ritual collaboration valid within (but not without) descent groups; or of the intercourse on an equal footing restricted to members of the same social stratum. We can visualize this discontinuous but repetitive distribution by representing the clusters of identical relationships (r) in the sub-groups, as against the relationships occurring at their boundaries (Br), in some such fashion:

$$\begin{bmatrix} rrr \\ rrr \\ rrr \end{bmatrix} Br \begin{bmatrix} rrr \\ rrr \\ rrr \end{bmatrix} Br \begin{bmatrix} rrr \\ rrr \\ rrr \end{bmatrix}$$

I suggest, then, that such distributive arrangements warrant special recognition, and that 'pattern' is an apt description.

---

[1] *The Division of Labour in Society*, transl. 1949, p. 175.

At the same time I do not propose to deal with them specifically in the subsequent discussion. Rather, I shall treat them as an unproblematic and relatively elementary aspect of social structure. They are unproblematic because there really is nothing further to be said about these patterns once we have described the repetitive distribution in question. And they are relatively elementary because a distributive order is the simplest kind of order, involving a very low level of abstraction. But we must note this. The distributive pattern never stands by itself; for if the respective subdivisions are in fact such, i.e. *components* of a society, then they must also be linked by certain interactions and by interrelations based on these: else they would not add up to one society (in which there must be behaviour 'towards and in regard to one another'). Thus the 'pattern' will go together with a 'network', and it is from the combination of the two that genuine problems will arise, the sort of problems we have in mind when we talk about the interdependence of group segments, about 'social symbiosis', or about the cohesion and integration of any 'society at large'.

By 'network', on the other hand, I mean the interlocking of relationships whereby the interactions implicit in one determine those occurring in others. Firth has recently commented on the fondness of anthropologists for metaphors like 'network', though he concedes the usefulness of this 'image' which allows us to visualize the relations between persons as 'links' and 'lines'.[1] Obviously, the network talked about by anthropologists is only a metaphor. But it has been used very effectively also by others, e.g. by physicists, engineers and neurophysiologists. They speak, for example, of communication networks or of the networks of nerve cells and paths. Let me stress that I am using the term in a very similar, technical sense. For I do not merely wish to indicate the 'links' between persons; this is adequately done by the word relationship. Rather, I wish to indicate the further linkage of the links themselves and the important consequence that, what happens so-to-speak between one pair of 'knots', must affect what happens between other adjacent ones. It is in order to illustrate this interrelatedness or interlocking of the relation-

[1] Raymond Firth, 'Social Organization and Social Change', *J.R.A.I.*, vol. 84, 1954, p. 4.

ships (each a 'link' between two 'knots'), that we require an additional term, and 'network' seems the most appropriate.

To mention another recent use of this metaphor. Barnes employs it to illustrate a particular kind of 'social field', constituted by relationships which spread out indefinitely rather than close in, as it were, and hence do not 'give rise to enduring social groups'. This spreading-out follows roughly the schema A*r*B, B*r*C, C*r*D . . . , though any one person may have relationships with several other persons and the 'other persons' may conceivably also maintain relations among themselves. A paradigm is friendship, each person seeing 'himself as at the centre of a collection of friends', who in turn have further friends and may or may not be friends with each other.[1] This picture comes close to the one I have in mind, though it represents a special and simpler case. For Barnes's 'network' does not predicate more than that certain relationships interlock through persons participating in more than one relationship; I visualize a situation in which this interlocking also bears on 'what happens' in the relationships and hence on their effective interdependence. For Barnes, the important thing is the dispersal of the relationships, and the open-ended character of the network; for me, its coherence and closure, that is, its equivalence with a 'system'.

(iv) Let me, in conclusion, say a little more about 'distributive patterns', more precisely about one particular type. It occurs when a society is so constituted that it contains a fixed number of subdivisions, of whatever kind. The fixed number only indicates the high degree of constancy characterizing the 'pattern'; and examples are of course familiar—societies having a moiety system, or six phratries (like the Zuni), four castes (like classical India), or so-and-so many age grades.

We might add that similar fixed numerical arrangements may apply also to the actors expected to fill particular roles or, more generally, to the population composing classes of people or sub-groups in the society. A club or association with a fixed membership and, perhaps, one President, two Vice-Presidents,

[1] J. A. Barnes, 'Class and Committee in a Norwegian Island Parish', *Human Relations*, vol. 7, 1954, pp. 43-4.

and three Members of Council, is a simple illustration. More sophisticated examples will be found in Simmel, who paid special attention to this aspect of social structure, considering it highly relevant.[1] Recently, from a somewhat different point of view, Lévi-Strauss has touched upon the same issue. He has in mind not a numerical arrangement fixed, i.e. kept invariant, by explicit social rules, but one exhibiting a purely statistical (and approximate) invariance.[2] This would be the case, if I may choose my own examples, where we find that the size of clans varies round a mean number, which is maintained by fission (if clans grow too large) or fusion (if they grow too small); or again, we might find that the ruling class in a stratified society always approximates to, say, ten per cent of the population.[3]

Now what is sociologically relevant in such numerical arrangements, whether they apply to persons in roles, to the population of sub-groups or to the number of the sub-groups themselves, is not the distributive pattern as such. Once more, considered by itself, it represents an unproblematic and elementary form of structuring. It becomes interesting and important only through its implication of interdependence between the persons or sections so numbered, that is, when it goes together with some differentiation and interlocking of their respective 'ways of acting' and hence with a 'network' of relationships. Thus the numbered set of phratries or castes may be so conceived that each has specific duties, secular or ritual, towards all others; a dual segmentation of the society, perhaps even the presence of two Vice-Presidents in an association, may serve to canalize and balance opposition; and the invariant population of clans or ruling classes may represent the optimum size for the particular activities assigned to these segments. Here we have a whole range of significant problems, and problems still in need of further study. They concern the extent to which these and similar forms of interdependence and integration depend on particular numerical arrangements or, conversely, the extent

---

[1] See *The Sociology of Georg Simmel*, ed. K. H. Wolff, 1950, pp. 105 ff.
[2] Op. cit., pp. 534-5.
[3] S. F. Nadel, 'Notes on Beni Amer Society', *Sudan Notes and Records*, vol. 26, 1945, pp. 16-17.

to which the numerical invariance facilitates (or the opposite) aimed-at possibilities of interaction. But these are essentially questions of adequacy, of the appropriateness of means to ends, that is, of *function*, and hence beyond the scope of this discussion.

II

PROBLEMS OF ROLE ANALYSIS

It should be stated, first of all, that the role concept is not an invention of anthropologists or sociologists but is employed by the very people they study. No society exists which does not in this sense classify its population—into fathers, priests, servants, doctors, rich men, wise men, great men, and so forth, that is, in accordance with the jobs, offices or functions which individuals assume and the entitlements or responsibilities which fall to them; in short, every society gives such linguistic notice of the differential parts individuals are expected (or 'briefed') to play. What anthropologists and sociologists have done over and above recognizing the existence of this categorization has been to turn it into a special analytical tool.

Its usefulness, in simplest terms, lies in the fact that it provides a concept intermediary between 'society' and 'individual'. It operates in that strategic area where individual *behaviour* becomes social *conduct*, and where the qualities and inclinations distributed over a population are translated into differential attributes required by or exemplifying the obtaining social norms. That this is a strategic area need not be especially emphasized; a great deal of sociological and social-psychological work deals with this crucial transition or translation. Nor is it difficult to show the need for such an intermediary concept. We have in fact already anticipated the logical gap which it is meant to bridge. Societies, though they are always composed of individuals, are not, strictly speaking, reducible to or divisible into individuals. For as we have said, societies rest on rules or norms and, consequently, on *constancies of behaviour* of various kinds, which we know as institutions or institutionalized modes of action, relationships, and groupings, and which we can further analyse into the constituent tasks, goals, expectations, rights and duties, and the like. All these, though they are exhibited in the behaviour (or conduct) of concrete individuals, are also independent of them. They function and continue to function with a personnel constantly reconstituted (ultimately by biological factors); and they involve the individuals not necessarily as entire human beings, but only with part of their individuality and certain of their qualities.

The concept needed to bridge the gap between society and individual must therefore refer, not to the concrete, unique human beings living and acting at any point of time, but to individuals seen as bundles of qualities: the qualities are those demonstrated in and required by the various tasks, relationships etc., that is, by the given, specified 'constancies of behaviour' in accordance with which individuals must act; while the 'bundle' corresponds to a class or type concept, including any or all individuals exhibiting the capacities in question. We can express more sharply the variability of the actor as against the constancy of the contribution expected of him by describing the latter as a part meant to be played. Which is precisely what the role concept is designed to do.

Historically, the conception of a theory of roles goes back to Pareto (1916) and Max Weber (1920). Pareto first recognized the sociological significance of the 'labels' we conventionally 'affix' to persons to indicate 'their proper place in the various classes' of people—labels such as 'lawyers, physicians, engineers, millionaires, artists'—though, for Pareto, this was no more than a step in the special analysis of social élites.[1] Weber, more generally and explicitly, outlined the methodological issues involved in such classifications of human beings. He argued that any empirical sociological analysis aimed ultimately at understanding, in terms of individual motives, how given types of society came into being and continue to exist, must be preceded by a 'functionally' oriented preliminary investigation. And there 'it is necessary to know what a "king", and "official", and "entrepreneur", a "procurer", or a "magician" does; that is, what kind of typical action, which justifies classifying an individual in one of these categories, is important and relevant for an analysis, before it is possible to undertake the analysis

[1] *The Mind and Society*, transl. 1935, §§ 2034-7.

itself.'[1] From about 1925 onwards the term 'role' appears more and more frequently in the writings of American sociologists such as W. I. Thomas, E. W. Burgess, and others. The first explicit formulation of the concept occurs, I believe, in the words of a philosopher (George Mead's *Mind, Self and Society*, 1934) and an anthropologist (Ralph Linton's *The Study of Man*, 1936). Since then it has been widely used by anthropologists, sociologists and psychologists, its most recent as well as most systematic treatment being due to Talcott Parsons and his collaborators.[2]

Recently, too, it has been argued that 'role' might not be the best term for the kind of phenomena it is meant to describe, mainly because of its dramatic and literary connotation and the 'figure-of-speech' use it encourages.[3] No better term, however, is suggested, though it is suggested that the existing term should be used in a stricter and more technical sense. I have no very strong feelings about the word 'role'; but I do share Newcomb's misgivings about the lax and often confused way in which it is handled. Altogether, role theory as it stands today still presents many unsatisfactory features, which can be cleared away, once more, only by rigorously re-thinking the whole problem.

2

As already indicated, the role concept is basically a type or class concept. Like the class concept of Logic it labels and brings together numbers of individuals—human beings in our case—in virtue of certain properties they have in common. The numbers obviously vary widely, between a substantial proportion of the population (all 'fathers', all 'old men') and one, as in 'unique' roles which can only have one representative at any one time (a 'sovereign', or perhaps an 'oldest member of the community'). Needless to say, there is no counterpart to the null-classes of Logic, which have no members at all. The role concept always refers to existing, real human beings; and if at any time a role

---

[1] *Principles of Social and Economic Organization* (transl. 1947), p. 97.
[2] Talcott Parsons, *The Social System*, 1951; Parsons, Shils and Bales, *Working Papers in the Theory of Action*, 1953.
[3] T. M. Newcomb, in *Social Psychology at the Crossroads*, ed. R. H. Roher and Muzafer Sherif, 1951, p. 36.

appears to be without a living representative, this will indicate only a temporary dislocation or anomaly.

In any class concept referring to human beings the properties underlying the classification may broadly be of two kinds. First, they may be physiological characteristics (sex, age, somatic features), qualities of descent and extraction, personality or character traits, or qualities resulting from some extraneous turn of events (as when we speak of a 'veteran' or a 'widow'). Secondly, the 'properties' may represent characteristic ways of acting, resting on particular proficiencies, interests or attitudes. This is not intended to be a full or systematic list of possibilities; but the twofold distinction is pertinent in that it separates attributes over which the individual has no control, being either inevitable or in some degree fortuitous (which I will call *contingent properties*), from others which he is free to assume and aim at (*achievement* properties).[1]

There are, however, certain special features which distinguish the role from the class concept. The latter is clearly the broader and looser of the two. The 'special features' narrow it down to a collective category which is not only applicable to human beings but sociologically relevant.

(1) *Ex definitione* the role concept has to do with behaviour, or differential behaviour, and the characteristics constituted by it. Even so, it may imply a reference to 'contingent' properties; such references ('old man', 'youth', 'brother', 'weakling') in fact often form the explicit criterion for classing individuals together. But the properties in question will never stand by themselves; rather they will be conjoined with others of a behavioural kind, in a manner to be discussed presently.

(2) Sociologically relevant behaviour is always behaviour towards or in regard to others. In the simplest case it conforms to the interaction model—'A behaves in a certain way towards B so that B responds in a certain way', and so on. Roles therefore materialize only in an interaction setting; consequently, the behavioural characteristics we have in mind when talking

[1] I am here using 'contingent' in a different though I think apter sense than I did in the *Foundations*, where I contrasted 'contingent' with 'vested' attributes or qualifications (op. cit. p. 152).

about roles will always include, besides the actor's own mode of behaviour, that of others towards him. In brief, the behavioural characteristics implicit in role concepts appear so to speak both in the *active* and *passive* voice.

(3) Sociologically relevant behaviour is always purposive; equally, it is repetitive, recurrent, having—as we have put it—some degree of 'constancy'. A given role, therefore, being made up of such behaviour exhibited in interaction settings, represents for other actors in their roles a set of data with which they can reckon and on which they can orient their own purposive actions. By itself, this condition could well apply to mere classes of people; for example, when a boxer knows that his opponent is a heavyweight and adjusts his style of fighting accordingly. But while the class concept refers merely to accidental, just-so likenesses which, however constant, could be quite otherwise, the role concept refers essentially to a lawful or *normative* conformity, in the sense that the shared attributes exhibited by individuals are understood to follow from the rules of the society or to involve them in some manner. More precisely, the individuals expect one another, and are expected by their society, to exhibit the attributes (knowingly and intentionally) as their allotted rights and obligations, entitlements or responsibilities.

(4) Finally, while the class concept requires the respective individuals to share only one property or attribute (which serves as the *differentia*, to use the phraseology of classical logic), the role concept requires the presence of a series of interconnected characteristics. Thus, if such names as 'priest', 'old man', or 'cyclist' were viewed merely as class concepts, they would indicate nothing beyond the fact that officiating in religious ceremonials, a ripe age, and devotion to cycling are properties shared by a number of individuals. As role concepts, these names indicate that further behavioural characteristics go with the *differentia*, and go with it 'normally', in consequence of the obtaining social rules. Though it may be difficult to think of 'cyclists' as a social role, being a 'priest' in this sense means that the individual who officiates in the religious ceremonies is also expected, say, to be of a certain age, to lead a decorous life, to enjoy an elevated status, and perhaps to forgo marriage; being

an 'old man' would similarly mean that a whole series of entitlements (or the opposite) and hence of expected ways of acting is entailed in mature age.

Certain comments are necessary. A word, first, on the methods involved when we define the rules or norms underlying a particular role. There are three interconnected methods, all familiar to the anthropologist or sociologist. They are in fact the general methods used in any investigation of social norms, resting respectively on frequency distributions, codification, and maintenance processes. The first method, then, is concerned with establishing the frequency and regularity with which the attributes assumed to make up the role appear together in fact, the result being the statistical 'normality' of the role series. The second method is concerned with the explicit statements and assertions of the people (made with a given degree of consensus and authoritativeness) as to the conduct appropriate to given roles; these are all value judgments, indicating the believed-in or desired 'normality', and hence the normality codified. Thirdly, the existing role norms are also demonstrated by what we may call the maintenance machineries of the society, that is, by the sanctions, of whatever kind, which forestall or follow deviant behaviour. Let us note that the first and third method involve the piecing-together of the role, while the second may furnish us with the total picture. For this and other reasons the three methods will not invariably give the same results. But for the sake of simplicity, and for the moment, we may ignore this.

Now my assumption that the role concept, unlike the class concept, refers to a whole series of attributes or characteristics and never to one only, needs some correction. Class concepts, too, though they might explicitly name one property only, have the implication of 'further' characteristics. But these would be entailed in the named property only as its material implications or consequences, as concomitants which cannot be 'thought away', as when the description 'a sick person' inevitably connotes incapacity for physical work, immobility, or dependence on the services of others. In role concepts, where the series of further characteristics is determined by the norms of the society, the entailment is essentially conventional and to that extent arbitrary, a different series being in theory possible. Thus where 'the sick' are a role, this will mean different things in different cultures—that the sick are entitled to special care or that they are exposed to neglect (because they are regarded as a burden), perhaps that they are treated as being particularly dear to the deity or are shunned as the bearers of a divine curse. The possibility or impossibility of 'thinking away' the particular implications of a name thus constitutes a further criterion in the distinction of class and role concepts.

Inasmuch as the 'further' characteristics can thus be 'thought away', they can also be expected to occur independently, without the crucial condition or conditions with which, by the social convention, they are normally linked. Differently put, people may simulate a role which is not really theirs, enacting it in the absence of the normal entitlement (though the 'simulation' might itself be legitimized by convention). It is in this sense that we say of a person that he stands *in loco parentis*, behaves 'as though he were the boss', or has usurped a certain status. In mere class concepts this separation of entitlement and conduct is meaningless. It would make no sense, for example, to say that so-and-so 'behaves as though he were a cyclist' or 'plays the part of a carpenter', though admittedly this additional linguistic test is not always as unambiguous.

This is due partly to the linguistic difficulty of distinguishing sharply between the mere simulation, say, of a physiological state ('he behaves as though he were a sick man') and the arrogation of the entitlements that go with it. But partly the ambiguity is due to the difficulty of finding unambiguous examples; for there are few human characteristics which are not, in some culture or society, elaborated into roles. In this sense class concepts, being broad labels based on any shared property, might be said to indicate the raw material from which roles are gained by the appropriate elaboration.

This, of course, is a matter of degree. And here another ambiguity arises; for the scale of elaboration may fail to bear out our premise that the role concept should provide a sociologically relevant categorization of human beings. In other words, we might be in two minds about accepting certain collective names as 'roles' (rather than as mere 'labels') if the attributes expressed in the names entail only small or unimportant series of 'further characteristics'. When I said before that it is difficult to think of 'cyclist' as a role I meant precisely this. Being a cyclist may well entail additional, purely conventional and normative attributes—a particular dress sanctioned by fashion, the obligation to ride on one side of the road or on special paths—and hence show some elaboration; but these characteristics would simply appear too inconsequential to warrant our speaking of a role. This does not mean that individual cyclists will not exhibit 'further' characteristics of some kind. But these would not be 'entailed' in being a cyclist; they would, as it were, be free qualities, not included in the elaboration or conventionalization of that category of human beings.

There are other examples illustrating the same point—'labels' referring broadly to origin or residence ('Londoner', 'townsman', 'Irish'), to minor talents and interests ('nature lover', 'bookworm'), or to more or less transitory conditions ('customer', 'patient', member of an 'audience'). It may similarly be doubtful if such descriptions as 'friend' or 'host' refer to roles proper, at least in societies where these positions are not conventionalized and in some degree 'elaborated'. A more important instance are the 'occupational roles' so-called. For they, too, may involve only a small-scale and relatively trivial conventionalization, referring to such things as working hours or working methods, 'tricks of the trade', perhaps a particular style of dress, or the appropriate conduct towards customers and fellow workers. Or the conventionalization, though not trivial, might only represent a useful routine adopted for its estimated efficiency, and hence a 'material consequence' of the occupation referred to in the role name.

Yet there are cases where the same kind of role will be elaborated more highly and as it were autonomously. Consider the blacksmiths in many primitive communities, who represent not just an occupational group, but an endogamous caste, credited with dangerous magic powers, and considered unclean or in other ways segregated from the rest of the community. Or we might think of the proverbial 'salesman', who is not only the representative of an occupation understood in a strictly technical sense, but something like a 'personality', being expected to be a 'jolly good fellow', boisterous and perhaps overbearing on all occasions, to frequent particular entertainments and belong to particular associations, and the like. For an illustration I can do no better than refer to the masterly description of the typical travelling salesman, the American version, in Theodore Dreiser's novel *Sister Carrie*.

Between the occupation which is only such and nothing else, and the one which represents conspicuously a role, there is clearly a fluid transition. This appears to go with the extent to which the 'further characteristics' spread beyond the narrow context of the occupational requirements as such. Borrowing a term from psychology we might say that the true occupational role, as indeed any true role, must have a *halo effect*.

What is a 'role', occupational or otherwise, without the halo effect? To be sure, it is reduced to a label or category. Yet in many cases it still labels or categorizes persons socially defined, occupying places in society which are governed by rules and circumscribed by institutional practices. It still represents, like the role proper, a 'brief', an 'occupancy' with rights and obligations, even though more narrowly or more technically based. There is this, too. The classes in which we may place persons vary widely in generality; and while a more specific class might only correspond to an 'occupancy', a more general one, subsuming the specific category, might indicate a role proper. Thus being a bank clerk, an insurance agent, or a postal official will hardly amount to a role as here understood; but being a white-collar worker probably will. The titles or ranks distinguishing members of an administrative organization usually indicate only difference in duty or office; but 'bureaucrat' is undoubtedly a role in the full sense of the word.[1] Since all distinctions of this kind are fluid ones, it seems unwarranted to insist on a sharp separation of roles proper from classes of persons not fully amounting to roles. Also, many of the things we shall have to say later will refer to both types of categorization. I shall therefore think of certain non-roles or near-roles as 'quasi-roles', and of our definition of social structure as including these also.

[1] Robert K. Merton, 'Bureaucratic Structure and Personality', in Kluckhohn and Murray, *Personality in Nature, Society and Culture*, 1950.

If it is felt that the quasi-roles ought to be specifically named, *status* seems an appropriate term. Used broadly, in a non-hierarchical and not necessarily jural sense, it describes precisely such mere 'briefs' or 'occupancies', i.e. particular sets of rights and obligations falling to persons. So understood, status is capable of being elaborated into roles, while all roles have a foundation in status. I confess to some dislike for this broad, Jack-of-all-trades use of status, which I would restrict to hierarchical position. What is more important, most writers on the subject couple roles and status in a different sense, considering them to be strictly complementary concepts, so-to-speak two sides of the same coin. To quote from Linton: 'There are no roles without statuses or statuses without roles', role representing 'the dynamic aspect of a status'.[1] Parsons argues on much the same lines. The role, he holds, is status translated into action, the role being the 'processual aspect' of status, as status is the 'positional aspect' of the role.[2] I doubt the value of this double appellation; indeed I consider it not only redundant but misleading.

It is relevant to emphasize, as Linton and Parsons have done, that in role behaviour something is translated into action. But the important thing about this 'something' is not that it is static or positional while the actual role is dynamic or processual; these are incidental features. The important thing is that in one case we have the execution of certain rights and obligations, that is, a *performance*, and in the other, this set of rights and obligations embodied in a piece of *knowledge*—in a norm or prescription, or perhaps only in an image people carry in their heads. In brief, we have a rule and its application. It seems unnecessary if not illogical to give different names to these two 'aspects'; for their coexistence is basic to every item of human acting that follows from rules. Each has this double identity (including, incidentally, our paradigm, the dramatic role proper), and could not be conceived without it.

There is a further point, however. Roles are never, strictly speaking, enacted all at once, being present so to speak in a piece. Rather, they are enacted phase by phase, occasion by

[1] *The Study of Man*, p. 114.
[2] *The Social System*, p. 25.

occasion, conceivably attribute by attribute, and hence in a 'process' extending over time. Only in the form of abstract knowledge are roles present as total entities, summarily 'positioning' the actors. Now the transition from the piecemeal performance to the total entity involves certain practical problems of perception and recognition. As we have mentioned, the investigator may in fact have to piece the role together. This is as true of the members of the society. Though they will not need to discover whether certain presumed roles really exist and how they are composed, they may still have to be certain about the particular roles involved in some situation in which they find themselves and which confronts them only with phases or facets of the total roles. The difficulties are resolved by the mutual entailment of the role attributes, which causes any one attribute to function as a cue for the others. Its perception by any interested person will indicate to him the presence or likely appearance of the further attributes in the series (provided, of course, he knows about the role composition); and it is thus that the 'mutual orientation' of actors upon each other's roles can materialize.

Not all attributes are equally good cues, either because they are not sufficiently exclusive to a given role or because they are not sufficiently firmly integrated ('entailed') in the series. But there are two special attributes whose function is exclusively that of providing cues or pointers. One consists in 'diacritical signs' implicit in role behaviour—fashions of dress, rules of etiquette, badges of rank, significant gestures and so forth, which are meant to distinguish persons in different roles and so to facilitate the perception of the latter. The second is the role name itself when used in forms of address or reference or in the form of titles to which people have a right. Even the simple introduction of a person as a 'priest', 'elder', as my 'mother's brother' or as my 'friend', is a cue or pointer conditioning the expectations of the listener. It should be noted that the role name here is part of the role behaviour and not only 'just a name', a point which will gain some importance later on.

The interaction settings or, more generally, the situations in which role behaviour materializes, will again differ in their cue values. For example, if I see a 'doctor' at the sickbed, a 'teacher' in the classroom, or a 'judge' in court, I shall be much more certain about the roles played by these actors than when I meet them in any other situation. This simply means that the appropriate performance of the roles requires a particular setting, which then conclusively proves (or disproves) their character. But not all roles have such a precise situational focus—think of such roles as 'old man', 'widow', 'pauper', 'friend'. Besides, we have assumed throughout the discussion that the true role is visible in a plurality of situations, its situational focus notwithstanding. And this happens in one of two ways. Either the same attribute will be manifest in numerous situations (the 'halo effect' mentioned before, as when a teacher is didactic in and out of school); or different attributes in the role series will come into play in different situations (as when a mother is expected to be loving at home but aggressive when it comes to defending her children against strangers). Thus the relation between role attributes and situations may be of a 'one-in-all' or of a 'one-to-one' kind. But the same role may include both kinds of attributes; nor does this distinction seem to be relevant in any other respect apart from its bearing on role perception.

3

We turn to a new question, the internal structure of roles. So far, the picture has been that of an interconnected series of attributes which, in their totality, make up the character of any given role. It is represented by the simple formula (ρ standing for 'role')—

(2) $$\rho = \Sigma\, a, b, c \ldots n.$$

The different attributes, however, are not all equivalent or of the same order. I shall try to show that any role series has a definite structure, of a hierarchical kind, in which the various attributes occupy places of graded relevance. We can distinguish three main grades.

(a) Certain attributes are peripheral in that their variation or absence does not affect the perception or effectiveness of the role which is being performed; in other words, they are understood to be optional or to admit of alternatives (like the married or unmarried status of doctors, poets or salesmen, but not, for example, of Catholic priests).

(b) Other attributes are sufficiently relevant, that is, sufficiently firmly entailed in the series, for their variation or absence to make a difference to the perception and effectiveness of the role, rendering its performance noticeably imperfect or incomplete. By 'making a difference' I mean essentially three things: the course of interaction provoked by the imperfect role performance will differ markedly from the usual, 'normal', course expected if the role is performed without variation; the interaction is likely to take the form of 'sanctions', i.e. of corrective, disapproving, or punitive behaviour (while the correct role performance is followed by facilitating or rewarding behaviour); and the imperfect role performance will evoke verbal criticism emphasizing its deviance from the norm, such as: 'she is not a proper wife' (perhaps because the woman in question does not look after a sick husband), or: 'he is not a proper artist' (perhaps because the individual referred to does not wear his hair long). It will be seen that these three 'differences' correspond (as they must, logically) to our three criteria of role norms—observed frequency, maintenance machineries, and evaluative statements (see pp. 23-4 above).

(c) The hierarchy of relevance culminates in attributes which are basic or pivotal in the sense that their absence or variation changes the whole identity of the role, and hence the interaction it would normally provoke (though there is the possibility that the complete role can be efficiently simulated). Structurally, the basic or pivotal attribute is such because, in its case, the role norm has zero tolerance. Its functional significance we have already anticipated: the basic or pivotal attribute is simply the attribute expected to entail the rest of the series. In normally entailing all the other attributes it also legitimizes them, so that, in its absence, the other attributes appear as illegitimate, unexplained, or with an altogether different meaning. Thus a woman who lives with a man and in every respect behaves as we should expect a wife to behave, without being married to him, is not a 'wife' but only 'as good as a wife'; and a man who wears his hair long and in all sorts of ways behaves like an 'artist', without ever having painted a picture, is not an artist, but, say, a 'bohemian'.

If we indicate the pivotal attribute by the sign p and the possibility of options or alternatives by the sign /, a total role might have this composition—

(3) $\qquad \rho = \Sigma\, p,\, a,\, b \ldots 1/m/n.$

We may note that a disproportionate number of optional attributes, reducing the firmly entailed (or 'relevant') attributes to very few, will produce the quasi-roles or mere 'statuses' discussed before (see above pp. 28-9). But the optional attributes can be more or less optional or 'free', being still subject to some rank order restricting the tolerance of the role; similarly, the second grade of relevance is likely to include further grades or steps. The precise ordering in this sense of all the attributes of a given role presents certain methodological problems, especially problems of scaling and ranking, which, at the moment, we may not be able to handle adequately or at least in any simple fashion. But these difficulties I will disregard. I must, however, insert some remarks about two other questions of method, since they bear directly on the procedure I now propose to follow. The first concerns the criteria for identifying the 'basic' or 'pivotal' characteristics of roles. The simplest and quickest way to decide what a role 'basically' means is to refer to the semantic content of the conventional role name, as I have done throughout and, more important, as I intend to go on doing. This method seems natural enough, since we cannot handle roles and intelligibly talk about them without calling them something. Indeed, it will often be the names current in a society for different classes or types of persons which first suggest to us the existence of the respective roles. The semantic approach is also legitimate since role names (like all class names) are shorthand symbols for the array of properties which the entity named is presumed to possess. In this sense the role name is prescriptive and stands directly for the role norm, with its given tolerance. I could also point out, again, that the role name is not 'just a name' but forms part of the behaviour concerned with roles and their norms, for example, when an incorrect role performance is sanctioned by the denial of the respective role name to the actor (a woman being refused the title of 'wife', a traitor that of 'citizen').

At the same time the use of verbal clues for the purpose of identifying the 'basic' attribute is reliable only if the linguistic usage is unambiguous, agreed, and consistent with the social practice; and to provide this kind of evidence is a complicated matter. But it does not always seem necessary; in certain cases the semantic structure of the role name itself seems to indicate the 'basic' attribute, in a way obvious to anyone capable of interpreting etymological clues. For a great many role names explicitly mention, in this obvious fashion, only one of the various role attributes, denoting the rest by tacit implication, thus suggesting that the property named is also the property most relevant or basic. Most examples so far quoted were of this kind. Furthermore, the grading of relevance suggested by the role names could be taken as being true in fact (an 'artist' being concerned primarily with producing works of art, an 'old man' being primarily old, whatever else may be expected of them). Admittedly, not every role name is thus informative; nor need the information, if it is conveyed by the name, be correct. The name 'elder', for example, might indicate, not primarily or necessarily old age, but tenure of a political or religious office. Again, the property indicated by the name might be less important or interesting than one tacitly implied, e.g. when the significant fact about 'blacksmiths' or 'sweepers' is that they are 'untouchables'. For the sake of convenience, however, I shall here assume that all the role names mentioned are of the simpler kind, having a correctly informative semantic structure, so that the property named can serve as a paradigm of the property 'basic' to the role. Properties fulfilling both these conditions I will call *governing* properties.

My second point concerns the very advantage in looking for a 'governing' property. For it could be argued that this is altogether irrelevant for the analysis of roles and should not be regarded as part of it but merely as a starting point. What is really interesting (the argument would run) about such roles as 'old man', 'wife' or 'artist' is not the criterion identifying them—old age, the marriage lines, concern with art—which can be taken for granted, but the 'further characteristics' that go with it. The viewpoint is implicit in several definitions of role advanced by social psychologists. They represent roles as 'patterns of behaviour' (or of relationships or 'expectancies') applying to persons 'occupying specific positions' or fulfilling 'definable functions' in the society;[1] the question 'Whence the position?' is not asked. The position or function is specified (by the conventional role name or in similar fashion) but otherwise disregarded; it merely provides the basis for enquiring into all the other attributes displayed by a person so described initially, the 'other attributes' being the proper subject matter for investigation.

As I see it, this viewpoint is legitimate in social psychology, concerned as it is with the interplay of social and psychological (or personality) factors. Thus it is also concerned, primarily, with the actual 'playing' of the roles in which individuals become involved in virtue of positions they happen to occupy or functions they undertake to fulfil; for it is here that attitudes, interests, and other personality traits or adjustments will above all be manifest. The question, 'Whence the position?' refers only to the given social conditions which set the whole process in motion, facilitating, hindering or generally shaping it, and can indeed be disregarded. For the anthropologist or sociologist, it is a crucial question. Since, as an anthropologist, I view roles as modes of acting 'allotted to individuals' by the norms of the society, I am concerned also with this very allocation and the principles on which it is based. Which means that my definition and analysis of roles must include their 'basis', the conditions entailing the 'further characteristics', as much as these characteristics themselves.

4

I must now show that this entailment can be of two kinds, or

[1] E. L. and R. E. Hartley, *Fundamentals of Social Psychology*, 1952, p. 486. Similarly T. M. Newcomb, in *For a Science of Social Man*, ed. John Gillin, 1954, pp. 253-4, and Muzafer Sherif, in *Social Psychology at the Crossroads*, 1951, p. 25.

can be pivoted in two different ways. This in turn depends on the character of the governing attribute—whether it is what I have previously called a 'contingent' or an 'achievement' property. We thus arrive at two important and in a sense complementary types of roles, and take the first step towards what is undoubtedly the most urgent task of role analysis, a taxonomy of roles.

In the first type of role, then, the governing property is an inevitable or fortuitous state in which individuals find themselves; it then entails the 'further characteristics'—all the other attributes in the series—as consequences or concomitants (as when mature age carries with it such-and-such privileges or responsibilities). In the second type of role, where the governing property is a behavioural attribute, active or passive, which individuals are free to choose as a goal or objective, the 'further characteristics' are entailed in it either as necessary preconditions or again as consequences and concomitants (as when priesthood requires celibacy and a decorous life, and promises an elevated status). Any antecedent condition upon which the assumption of all the other role attributes depends operates as a principle of recruitment for the role in question. In this sense the first type of role is identified by a governing property which also indicates the method of recruitment; it may thus be called a *recruitment role*. In the second type of role, which is by contrast an *achievement role*, the recruitment is implicit in the 'preconditions'. In either case the fulfilment of the antecedent conditions belongs, strictly speaking, to the prehistory of the role, to the phase of its assumption rather than its actual performance; and the crucial steps may be concentrated in a formal procedure meant to demonstrate either the fulfilment itself (as in tests, examinations and the like) or the successful role assumption (as in ceremonials of induction). But what happens in the prehistory of the role is likely to remain important also in the phases of the role performance, as when the qualities which led to the recruitment will be expected to last through the lifetime of the role.

Roles having such a relevant prehistory might in fact appear to constitute a special type, having two instead of one 'basic' attribute. One of these would refer to the conditions of recruitment and their fulfilment or non-fulfilment: as when a medical practitioner without a degree or diploma is not a 'doctor' but a 'quack'. The other, to some feature considered crucial in the performance of the role: as when a 'doctor' who does not treat patients is not a 'real 'doctor, i.e. the medicating kind (which the French term *médicin* and the German term *Arzt* name specifically). I suggest, however, that in most, perhaps all, cases of this kind one of the two 'basic' attributes will prove to belong to the second grade of relevance (see p. 32 above), so that our assumption of a single governing attribute need not be qualified.

We can express this internal structure of roles schematically, with the help of a few additional symbols: $\rightleftarrows$ shall stand for 'entailment '(antecedent and consequent respectively); p again for 'governing property'; a, b ... m, n for the 'further characteristics'; t for the time at which role behaviour is assumed or exhibited and $\pm$ for any modification of t; and r for 'recruitment'. Then, in the first type of role

(4) $\qquad \rho_1 = \Sigma p$, a, b ... m, n
$\qquad$ if $p^t \longrightarrow$ (a, b ... m, n)$^{t+}$
$\qquad$ and $p = $ r.

In the second type of role

(5) $\qquad \rho_2 = \Sigma p$, a, b ... m, n
$\qquad$ if (a, b ...)$^{t-} \longleftarrow p^t \longrightarrow$ (m, n)$^{t+}$
$\qquad$ and (a, b ...) $=$ r.

It will be seen that in the case of recruitment roles (ρ_1) the individual is forced into the given role or at least compelled to a restricted choice; in achievement roles (ρ_2), he 'embraces' the role for its desirability, voluntarily committing himself to its various implications. This distinction is related to but does not coincide with the familiar dichotomy of *ascribed* and *achieved* status. Achievement roles mean much the same as achieved status (ignoring the looser meaning of 'status'). But the concept of ascription does not cover the case of recruitment roles as here understood. The ascription of status is usually taken to indicate the investment of persons with distinct offices or roles on the grounds of some quality over which they have no control, especially birth, sex, and age; I mean, by recruitment roles, the elaboration into roles of these qualities themselves. In the first case, then, we have generally important duties and privileges reserved, say, for persons of gentle birth, for young men and old men, for males and females; and I shall have more to say about these roles a little later. In the second case, we have the very roles 'gentry', 'youths', 'the aged', and perhaps 'man' and 'woman' in general. Again, in the first case we may speak, with Parsons, of roles being 'allocated to actors';[1] but in recruitment roles this allocation turns into something else, namely, into *accommodation*, the society acknowledging and absorbing, that is, providing legitimate niches for, the variety of human beings within it. It will be seen that the principle of accommodation extends beyond the ubiquitous biological differences of birth, age, and sex; it applies equally, and even more clearly, on the border zones of normality, underlying such roles as the sick, sexual perverts, cowards and heroes, imbeciles and geniuses.

The principle of allocation operates in the opposite sense in achievement roles. Here, where the society holds certain roles available for intending actors, we may speak, once more with Parsons, of 'the allocation of personnel' to roles and of the 'flow of personnel within the role system'. The desirability, i.e. the achievement character, of the roles is the incentive making the allocation possible and thereby ensuring that needed roles are in fact filled. To think of roles in terms of allocation is to think of them in economic terms, the underlying idea being that of given social requirements met from the available human resources. It was Pareto, incidentally who first expressed this 'economic' aspect of role systems.[2] As I suggested, it is one-sided, and must be supplemented by that other aspect or principle, of accommodation.

The two will often overlap, mainly because the contingent qualities of individuals also include gifts and capacities which the society will wish to utilize as well as accommodate. Perhaps, too, there are roles which fit in neither category (brother-in-law, enemy, bureaucrat). They simply exist or develop, and it would be futile to try and explain them on the grounds of allocation or accommodation. The only possible explanation would be near-

[1] *The Social System*, p. 117.
[2] *Mind and Society*, §§ 2044-5.

tautological, in terms of that basic tendency to regularize rights and obligations which is part of social existence itself. Yet though the explanatory power of the two principles is limited, they remain relevant; for to dismiss them would mean accepting the randomness of role systems or stipulating nothing more precise than the trivial truth that 'societies are like that'. Nor can we deny that, in any concrete situation, the allocation of roles is demonstrated by the various procedures for replacement, succession, training etc., and accommodation, by all the human differences, including unusual ones, which are in effect legitimized by congenial roles.

Let me return to our two categories, *recruitment* and *achievement* roles, and briefly consider certain complications and transitional forms. A few roles may be viewed in either light. This is true of kinship roles such as father, mother, husband and wife. For it is clear that a person may desire to be a parent (i.e. have a child) or to marry, and that he can take practical steps to achieve this end; at the same time, there is an element of accident about the former and—in certain societies—an element of compulsion about the latter. In other kinship roles the achievement aspect, though not logically excluded, is in practice ruled out. It seems extremely unlikely that anyone will particularly want to be a brother-in-law or a father's sister or that, even if the desire were there, he or she could take any practical steps about it. Here as in all roles implying offspring position, the role is simply the consequence of procreation and descent (one's own or somebody else's).

I regard ascriptive roles (or 'ascribed statuses') as another transitional form. For in essence they are concealed and (or) attenuated recruitment roles. Their names identify them as achievement roles and, like the latter, they are focused upon a particular function or position which is understood to 'entail' such-and-such preconditions. But these would include contingent properties, so that the role has some of the compulsive or restrictive character of recruitment roles. The degree of compulsion will vary: the person possessing the contingent qualities may be automatically recruited to the given role; or the respective preconditions may merely restrict eligibility. There is no need to give examples. It is worth noting, however, that the 'concealment' of the compulsive or restrictive aspect of these roles is only due to their insufficiently informative names, such as 'soldier', 'priest', or 'noble' (instead of 'conscript', 'hereditary priest' or 'noble by descent').

Linguistic usage will do justice to the distinction even though it may not be semantically expressed. Nor need explicit semantic expressions be absent. An interesting example is the Nupe name for a special priest recruited (compulsorily) on the grounds of a rare accident of birth; he is known as 'The Rare Man', while ordinary priests are known simply as 'The Men who Sacrifice'.[1] We might speculate on the consequences of a linguistic usage which would in every respect be correct and informative. 'Ascribed' roles would then disappear, being replaced by (correctly named) recruitment roles. But it seems that societies do not particularly care for such frankness; in the case of numerous roles they prefer the illusion of achievement, however small its real chances.

Considering achievement roles in the full sense of the word, we must note that the 'achievement' itself has a wide and flexible meaning. For example, individuals will commit themselves to playing particular roles not because the whole role is attractive, nor yet for the sake of the governing property; rather they may do so for the sake of some other attribute in the series, which is the one they consider desirable. Thus a man might enter the Church not because he feels 'called' but because this position offers security as well as elevated status; or he might strive to be an 'artist' merely because the bohemian life appeals to him. Again, individuals may drift or slip into roles unawares, having in some respect acted in the characteristic fashion without calculating the full commitment (as when a 'lover' suddenly discovers that he is regarded as a 'suitor', a man of initiative finds himself an acknowledged 'leader', and others have 'greatness thrust upon them').

This type of situation has considerable relevance in law, though there, of course, one does not speak of 'features' of roles as against the 'full' commitment implicit in them, but rather holds the *de facto* conduct of individuals against the jural status which this conduct would normally signify. Thus the

[1] S. F. Nadel, *Nupe Religion*, 1954, p. 72.

English concept of *estoppel* implies that a person might be required to show reason why he should 'stop' at certain responsibilities pertaining to a particular status when his behaviour in other respects can be presumed to establish that status.

5

Our last topic bears on a much wider problem. We were describing something in the nature of pre-role behaviour which, at that stage, is purely individual and idiosyncratic, and only later becomes conduct typical of roles. Perhaps we have, throughout this discussion, tended too much to argue as if societies permitted hardly any significant behaviour which was not also role behaviour. If so, the last remarks should correct this impression. Obviously, individuals do also act as individuals, frequently and with all the idiosyncrasies that go with this way of acting. But 'purely individual' behaviour yet takes place within the ever-present setting of role categories and conventions, and cannot but be affected by them. This means several things, most of them familiar and often mentioned. It means, for example, the chance that individuals may find fully congenial roles, accommodating all their leanings and peculiarities; it means the chance of playing a given role in an individual manner, through utilizing (or exceeding) its tolerance; and it means, also, the power of certain enduring roles to remodel the personality of the players. Let me stress only that further possibility, of individual behaviour being caught up in the role matrix, in the manner discussed a moment ago. Indeed, certain roles seem to allow specifically for this transition between pre-role and role behaviour: think of neighbourliness which may develop into the conventionalized conduct expected of 'neighbours'; of friendliness turning into (institutionalized) friendship, or of personal antagonism forcing the individuals into the position of recognized 'enemies'.

We may thus compare role assumption with a set of rules, rules of a game as it were, which come into operation whenever an individual shows evidence of wishing to play the game in question or of having in fact started to play it. The same model also illustrates most other features of role behaviour. The rules of the game have a given latitude, allowing certain options and disallowing others, with varying degrees of strictness; some 'moves' are altogether excluded since they would simply change or deny the identity of the game—which is the exact counterpart of our 'hierarchy of relevance'. The overall firmness with which the whole set of rules applies corresponds to the institutionalization of the roles in the social system; and as in all institutionalizations, the respective expectations are diffused through the society. In other words, the rules of the game are known to and reckoned with by the intending players. Miscalculations and misconstructions do happen; but given moves also operate as cues foreshadowing subsequent moves, and there may be special conventions turning particular moves into 'pointers' proper. Finally, as in many games played according to rules, the moves open to the players, that is, the attributes they are expected to acquire or display, will follow a more or less rigorous sequence, so that a particular attribute must not appear or will not be effective unless some other specified attribute is already present.

In a broad sense, this sequential aspect was implicit in our distinction of 'preconditions' and 'consequences'. It is easy to see that it may apply also to items among the preconditions. We are familiar with the progressive acquisition of different qualifications, or with rules of precedence governing different entitlements (as when wealth is an entitlement to upper class status only in addition to being of 'good family'). But the sequential character of roles extends beyond role assumption and recruitment to the actual playing of roles; and there it characterizes a type of role not yet fully discussed.

Certain roles have no precise hierarchy, there being no definite focus or pivot in the series. Nor are they triggered off by any event or quality operating as a precise principle of recruitment. Consistent with this, the role names usually make no reference to any 'governing' attribute, but indicate the role character in a generalizing, summary fashion ('friend', 'enemy', 'lover', 'patriot'). The only structure which these roles possess lies in the more or less clearly prescribed sequence of attributes, which becomes visible as the role is being played, as it develops and so-to-speak unfolds. For example, though 'friends' (in our own society) may express their enactment of that role in numerous ways, none having logical primacy over the other, it is unlikely that among their early acts will be that of borrowing money from one another; rather, this act will be normal only if there have been some previous other expressions or tokens of friendship. Again, the non-formalized leadership in many primitive societies requires the leader to be a sympathetic listener to complaints and a tactful manager of delicate social situations before he can begin to command and 'lead'. Roles of this third type can be defined by this formula:

(6) $$\rho_3 = \Sigma\ a, b, \ldots n,\ \text{if (say)}\ a^t \longrightarrow n^{t+}.$$

The problem of developing or unfolding roles and their sequential aspects still needs a great deal of further study. Certain experiments of Bales and his collaborators, concerned with the gradual fixation of roles in group situations, closely bear on this issue (see p. 114). But we also need field studies applying this approach to the institutionalized procedures of 'real' groups. I do not propose to say very much more about it save that it seems to me extremely important and promising. It would elucidate, for example, that fluid transition from pre-role to role behaviour, which is only a variant of the 'unfolding' of roles. In some measure, moreover, the sequential aspect is common to all roles, even those hierarchically arranged and triggered-off by precise rules of recruitment. There, it shows the optional periphery of roles in a new perspective. The latitude to assume or neglect certain attributes or to choose between alternatives may prove to be more than merely a given 'degree of tolerance', namely a decisive condition for the further development of the role.

Take this example from my own field (slightly simplified for the sake of the argument). A Nupe 'father' may or may not have his adult sons in his labour team, and he may or may not pay their bride price when they marry. But of the four possible combinations of these two options, the third never occurs, thus:

Sons in labour team	Paying bride price
+	+
+	−
−	+
−	−

∼ (spanning rows 3)

In other words, the attribute 'readiness to pay the son's bride price' will not appear unless the attribute 'running a labour team including the son' is already present. More generally speaking, such roles will develop in a certain direction through being, at a previous stage, 'played' one way rather than the other. The respective formula would read, for example:

(7) $$\rho_4 = \Sigma\, p,\, a/b,\, c/d \ldots \text{if}$$
$$a^t \longrightarrow c^{t+},$$
$$b^t \longrightarrow d^{t+}.$$

We may here speak of a principle of *linked options*. But this principle bears on a much wider issue—the very interaction setting in which all roles materialize. For the option made by an actor in the course of his role performance, which determines the subsequent development of the role, is likely to be itself determined by the previous responses he encountered on the part of his co-actors. Thus we must accept something in the nature of a *mutual steering process* whereby the performance of one role guides or conditions the performance of another. We shall return to this point when discussing the 'maintenance processes' which ensure correct role behaviour and check tendencies to deviance.

III

CONFORMITY AND DEVIANCE

I MUST now correct a final over-simplification in the previous discussion. I spoke throughout of the social norms behind role behaviour as though for each role there were only one unequivocal norm. This is obviously untrue. We know that diverse and even conflicting social norms frequently coexist in the same society, being valid for different strata of the population, different ages and generations, or the two sexes, and what is true of social norms in general is likely to be true also of the norms underlying roles. I did imply that in defining the character of roles we assume some degree of variability; I referred to the frequency distribution of role attributes, and I pointed out that in eliciting statements about roles we must reckon with a 'given degree of consensus'. But we may legitimately ask how far the frequency distribution will be such that we can define a 'normal distribution', and hence speak of a 'typical' father, doctor, or artist? And whether the consensus will always be sufficient to permit us to talk once more about what happens 'normally' or 'typically'? Though these questions can be fully answered only for the concrete case, certain general remarks can be made.

If the distribution of attributes which we presume, or perhaps only suspect, to belong to a certain role is indeed completely irregular, that is, if all the attributes prove to be optional ones, then obviously our presumption was unfounded and no roles of the assumed kind exist. But equally obviously, our presumption must have had some foundation. I have suggested that, often, it is the existence of names describing classes of people which makes us think of roles. (Perhaps, too, having read books about role behaviour has further predisposed us towards this way of thinking.) But the most important clues are probably the assertions of the people we study, the fact that they will argue how 'fathers' or 'priests' behave or should behave, and how others behave or ought to behave towards them. It is not impossible that a more careful study and the use of a better sample of informants will show the consensus to be much weaker than we first assumed. Perhaps it will prove altogether insignificant, or it will indicate some degree of uncertainty of judgment, showing the role norm to be to that extent ill defined. In practice this might mean that the role considered reverts to a mere class of people, defined by a particular attribute entailing no 'further characteristics' with any measure of predictability.

Even so, I feel that initial assumptions about the presence of roles are always justified and heuristically useful. They have the usefulness of all assumptions about constancies in enquiries such as ours, which are, after all, concerned with establishing the norms and regularities of social life. If the assumptions do nothing else, they will warn us not to cede too much ground, or to cede it too quickly, to the mere biographies of individuals.

The uncertainties of judgment I mentioned a moment ago may well reflect a phase of change and transition. Perhaps new roles are crystallizing while public opinion is still confused as to their precise import. I have given an example elsewhere; it concerns the new role of 'merchant prince' in Nupe, where wealthy men of the merchant class had only recently been admitted to the titled nobility and it was as yet impossible to predict in what fashion these two characters might eventually merge.[1] Again, the change may be in the opposite direction, so that firm combinations of attributes previously required would be loosened and the requirement itself cease to have an agreed meaning. As a result the role name would become a historical relic and the actor in the role a semi-mythical creature, to wit, that famous quasi-role, the English gentleman. It is undoubtedly true to say that 'one of the features of our own time is the indeterminacy and rapid changing of roles'.[2]

Yet we should beware, I think, of regarding all fluid, badly defined roles too readily as indicative of change, especially of change tending towards the weakening of norms and states of 'anomie'. For roles even in their pristine conceptions may be of such a fluid type, and socially useful because of that. They would

---

[1] *A Black Byzantium*, 1942, pp. 98, 365.
[2] W. J. H. Sprott, *Social Psychology*, 1952, p. 155.

still be roles proper, with a core, although a small one, of firmly interconnected characteristics: but these serve to legitimize further qualities intentionally left undefined and even unpredictable. The eccentricity accepted in poets, artists, or millionaires (but not in school-teachers or members of the middle class) is a trivial example. A more significant one is the role of prophets and visionaries, religious or secular, of leaders given *carte blanche* as to where they will lead you, and of other persons legitimately embodying what Max Weber has called 'charisma'.

The emphasis is on 'legitimately'. For the contrast so often drawn, and formulated most sharply by Weber, between the 'charismatic' leader whose position is 'by its very nature' non-institutional, and other leaders whose position rests on 'ordered procedures' and a 'regulated career', seems to me to omit an important intermediary type.[1] I have referred to it very briefly in my *Foundations* when I spoke of the possibility that even charismatic efforts can be 'routinized' and re-absorbed into the institutional life of the society.[2] I would now express it somewhat differently. I would say that societies provide such roles in order to accommodate certain unpredictable personalities and, more important, in order to sanction and utilize their irregular, unexpected or revolutionary inspirations. These are, once more, developing and unfolding roles; and what their stable 'core' does is to ensure the freedom of this unfolding.

To return to the instances showing changing and disintegrating roles. We have assumed that in such circumstances our attempts to construct roles and define role norms may face a double failure, in that both the distribution of role attributes and the consensus as to their relevance will fail to produce any 'typical' or 'normal' picture. Is perhaps a 'single' failure as likely? Can we assume that, sometimes, the assertions about what a role ought to be are precise and uniform, and only its enactment confused or divergent? I doubt if a strict conflict of this kind ever occurs. Take the very common case of a precisely formulated role norm going together with relatively few and irregular instances of deviance. It is at least likely in the circumstances

---

[1] Max Weber, *Essays in Sociology*, ed. H. H. Gerth and C. Wright Mills, 1948, pp. 246, 248.
[2] Op. cit. p. 190.

that the people behaving in the deviant fashion will agree that they are in the wrong and that their behaviour in fact infringes the accepted norm, whose validity is not being called in question. But if the deviance is widespread and frequent, we should expect the nonconformists to defend their conduct. They could do so only by insisting that their reading of the situation, of their own rights and obligations, in brief, of their roles, is the correct one, even though opposed to that of their critics. Which means that their assertions would break the common consensus as their actions break the presumed norm.

But let us be clear that here we have not simply uncertainty about what a role really means, but the coexistence of diverse beliefs and believed-in norms. And in such an event consensus or its opposite is not the only evidence we should adduce. We should consider also the degree of authoritativeness with which the respective assertions are made. In other words, we should take into account the varying qualifications of the people expressing the conflicting views and the extent to which they may be said to speak 'on behalf of the society'. If this criterion can be applied, we should know who is the nonconformist and who is not, who upholds a common value and who propounds, if not a minority view, at least one that is illegitimate. This, of course, means presupposing the character of certain roles in order to ascertain the 'correct' character of others. More precisely, we must be able to reckon with roles implying the authority to legislate on all sorts of other roles.

Though no one is likely to quarrel with this assumption, circular though it may seem, there are other difficulties. For occasionally the 'authoritativeness' may be even on either side. People belonging to different social strata, age groups, and so forth may each maintain their own interpretation of roles of common concern, with equal claims to legitimacy. The rich may maintain that wives should not work and the poor that they should; and the wives may have their own ideas about this. More important, the people holding the opposed views may hold them about one another, and may even each concede that the other side has a right to its peculiar views. Paradoxically speaking, the plurality of norms may itself be considered 'normal', so that it is expected by the actors in their conduct towards one another. Doctors usually have their own ideas about the proper behaviour of patients, but will probably admit that few patients live up to that role. Or to quote a less trivial example, fathers might expect their sons (and sons their fathers) to act from notions about parental and filial rights and obligations which are opposed to their own; and Society (or its spokesmen) might concede this to be the 'normal' state of affairs.

The concession to plural standards, however, has strict limits. Beyond them lie, first, the evaluative judgment about imperfect role performances mentioned before and secondly, evaluating judgments indicating not only the imperfection of the role performance but its undesirable or noxious character. The latter judgments may still be expressed by way of criticism only—a 'bad' father or son, a 'dishonest' doctor or businessman; that is, they do not indicate the presence of special, disapproved roles, but merely deviance from an approved one. At the same time certain forms of deviant behaviour are also positively expressed, suggestive of roles proper, though disapproved ones, whether these refer summarily to individual conduct (a 'criminal', a 'sceptic') or to specific actions and even occupations considered undesirable ('rebel', 'prostitute', 'deserter'). By our definition they *are* roles if they have the stipulated 'halo effect' and if the respective behaviour is such, for example, that individuals can 'slip' into it, being in consequence committed to all the 'rules of the game'.

But from another point of view such deviancy roles, if we accept them, fail to fit our original definition, which referred to role behaviour as dictated by the obtaining social norms and as representing rights and obligations allotted to individuals. For being a criminal, rebel or deserter is clearly neither a right nor an obligation, though some such deviant 'roles' might exist by tacit concession, in virtue of permissive rights (as when a society allows prostitution or scepticism, e.g. as regards religion). In either case, however, the society will reckon with the deviance from norms and will, in its norms, provide for corrective, punitive or retaliatory counter-measures. Thus rights and obligations *are* involved in these situations, though they devolve on the people responding to the deviant behaviour, affecting the deviant actor himself only passively. Above all, rights and obligations are also involved in the sense that they provide the foil and measuring stick for deviant roles; for the deviant role is such because it negates obligations and exceeds rights or functions in their absence. The deviancy role, we might say, is a role with a negative coefficient.

There is, finally, a borderline case which in a sense tests this whole presumed readiness of people to think of one another in terms of roles, including roles beyond the range of morality. I spoke a little earlier jokingly of semi-mythical roles. Now a case can be made out for the existence of mythical roles in the strict sense of the word. I am thinking of certain types of sorcerers and witches in primitive societies. The consensus of opinion on how these beings behave, what they do, what characteristics they have, and what others will do when meeting with them, is often extremely high. Often, too, the concrete, tangible attributes ascribed to sorcerers or witches will fall in a precise series, very much like the role series we have been discussing; which point I have illustrated for the witchcraft beliefs of Nupe.[1] Furthermore, these tangible properties are regarded as so many 'pre-conditions'; only when they are present does one assume that the other, intangible, *magic* properties will also appear or must appear. It is, of course, these magic characteristics which represent the 'pivotal' features, the 'governing properties', of these quasi-roles; and they are purely mythical or mystical. The role itself, therefore, has no reality. But the conceptions involved do prove that this way of thinking about human (or near-human) beings, as 'bundles' of qualities interconnected in some lawful fashion, stops at the boundaries of the supernatural and irrational as little as it stops at the boundaries of the immoral.

2

The question how role performances are kept from deviance and within the boundaries of conventional morality, belongs to a treatise on social control. But any role performance, set as it is in an interaction context, also has built into it certain elements of control or, more precisely, of 'self-regulation' as I have called

[1] See *Nupe Religion*, 1954, chap. VI.

it.[1] These can be demonstrated and explained with the help of another model—Talcott Parsons's schema of interaction, which, using a fashionable analogue, we might in turn describe as a simple 'feed-back' model.

Parsons argues that the expectations guiding the role behaviour of any actor must always be dichotomous, corresponding to the duality implicit in any interaction setting. Thus any actor will have certain notions concerning his own behaviour in the given role, which include the current 'definitions of how its incumbent should act towards others': these are his 'role-expectations'. At the same time the actor will also have expectations 'relative to the contingent probable reactions of others': these are, from his point of view, 'sanctions' of his behaviour, punitive or rewarding. These two sets of expectations are always reciprocal in that 'what are sanctions to ego are role-expectations to alter and *vice versa*'. In consequence there will be a mutual steering of behaviour resting on this 'complementarity of expectations' about how the given roles are to be played. And since the respective expectations normally refer to 'common standards of value-orientation', to institutionalized 'shared value patterns', the mutual steering will have the effect of maintaining these, that is, of preserving the obtaining role norms. Any tendency to deviance on the part of one actor will be met and corrected by the punitive sanctions provided by the other; conformity or 'normality' will in turn be rewarded and hence reinforced.[2] Which is a strict parallel of the efficacy of 'positive' and 'negative' feed-back.[3]

It is obvious that this dyadic model with its strictly reciprocal operation can readily be extended to include also more complex and indirect control effects: thus A may modify his role-playing *vis-à-vis* B not only because of B's 'sanctioning' reactions, but because a third party C intervenes in some such fashion. But we may for the moment disregard this extension which does not materially affect the problem under discussion. Again, we must not think of the control effects too narrowly, as always depending

[1] See 'Social Control and Self Regulation', *Social Forces*, vol. 31, no. 3, 1953.
[2] Talcott Parsons, *The Social System*, pp. 38-40.
[3] See Norbert Wiener, *Cybernetics*, 1948, pp. 114-15; *The Human Use of Human Beings*, 1950, pp. 12-14.

on reactions that can properly be described as 'rewards' or 'punishments', or as 'gratification-promoting' and 'depriving'. Nor is the intention behind the sanctions a crucial condition. All that is required for these effects to arise is that there should be 'meaningful reactions of alter to what ego does', and that each actor should 'care how others react to him.'[1] Thus if alter responds to ego's behaviour (because this happens as expected) merely by facilitating or not hindering ego's intentions, this will already reinforce ego's notion as to how to play his role; and if alter, in response to ego's 'deviant' behaviour, merely does something for which ego does not 'care', this is likely to check and conceivably correct ego's rendering of the role.

Effects of this kind are too obvious and familiar to need illustration. Yet though the model is so persuasive, it is unsatisfactory in certain respects. To begin with, it seems to me unwarranted to separate, as Parsons does, the set of expectations ego has concerning his own role (and which are more appropriately called his 'role knowledge') from his expectations concerning alter's reactions. It is surely absurd to say that I as a 'patient' have one set of notions about how to behave towards a 'doctor', and another about how a doctor is likely to behave towards me. Rather, the knowledge I have of my own role inevitably includes assumptions about the reactions of others in their roles. Furthermore, these assumptions must on occasion be wrong, in spite of the general condition implicit in Parsons's model that ego and alter share a common 'value pattern'; otherwise, there could never be a case of deviance, and the 'sanctions' would never need to be corrective. Nor, finally, is it enough to say that what is role knowledge for alter becomes sanctions for ego. The sanctions would not be sanctions but arbitrary or illegitimate responses unless ego is also informed about alter's role and accepts alter's understanding of it, with all its consequences for ego's own behaviour. Thus if my 'doctor' blames or praises my morals or otherwise tries to influence my private life, I shall probably dismiss his intervention as irrelevant or presumptuous since I do not take this kind of interest to be part of his job. Similar reactions on the part of a friend, relative, clergyman or magistrate might weigh with me, and operate as 'sanctions',

[1] Talcott Parsons, op. cit. pp. 40, 41.

ROLE CHART

Recruitment roles		Achievement roles			
Independently defined	*Dependently defined*	*Independently defined . . . . . . Dependently defined*				*Relational roles*	
	Relational roles	*Proprietory roles*	*Expressive roles*	*Service roles*		
1	2	3	4	5	6	7
On the basis of—somatic features, age, sex, personality, extraction, origin, descent, kinship etc.	Kinship roles	Roles indicating possession of skills, resources, learning, etc.	Belief roles, creative roles (e.g. 'artist'), communication roles (e.g. 'orator')	So-called 'occupational roles'	Symmetrical: membership roles, partnership roles, rivalry roles	Asymmetrical: managerial roles, authority, leadership roles, hierarchical ('status') roles, patronage roles, etc.

since I understand and agree that such concern (or 'care') is legitimate in their case.

More generally speaking, any successful corrective act is such only because the individual corrected is prepared to concede that the corrector is acting legitimately, in pursuance of his proper role; and any corrective act which is dismissed or rejected suffers this fate because one denies that the other person's role legitimizes the conduct in question. Much the same goes for any action reinforcing conduct, by facilitation, praise or reward, though admittedly such gratifying responses are much less likely to be examined for their legitimacy.

Now all this is again quite obvious. Is it not also irrelevant? In a sense, we were only spelling out Parsons's broader premise, that alter's reactions must be 'meaningful' to ego; and, going further than Parsons, we also specified the conditions under which this 'meaning' fails to operate. But is this contingency really important? The 'meaning' which one actor must find in the sanctioning behaviour of the other derives from the given, common standards and institutionalized 'value patterns'. Thus, if one actor rejects that meaning, that is, denies the sanctioning potentialities or implications of his fellow actor's role, he also rejects the value pattern, the social norm altogether. Assuming this to be a genuine rejection and not simply another error to be corrected in due course, it would seem to indicate only a fortuitous, idiosyncratic negativism, say, a person's obstinate refusal to agree with the majority. The possibility of such idiosyncratic acts occurring is undoubtedly real enough; but it would be irrelevant from our point of view, since we are, after all, concerned with the norms of role behaviour and not with fortuitous denials of them. Parsons's model has to do with 'the conditions of relatively stable interaction in social systems', implying defined 'value standards' and 'institutionalized role expectations'; any wilful disagreement with them simply falls outside the stipulated stability and the model based on it.

I would argue that this is not necessarily so and that our model must allow for such disagreements. Even 'relatively stable' social systems do not exclude them, or include them only in the form of purely fortuitous contingencies. Far from being fortuitous or idiosyncratic, the rejection of the sanctioning potentialities of other roles may itself be anchored in the existing institutions, reflecting the presence of diverse but equally legitimate 'value patterns', ideologies or schools of thought, that is, that plurality of norms we spoke of before. Think only of the conflicting views about their respective roles which may characterize father and son generations: a son will then be unmoved by his father's praise or censure of his conduct if he believes that his father's (as all fathers') pretension to authority is unjustified or out of date. Thus our point concerning the assumptions which one actor must have about the role of the other remains important. To sum up, the mutual steering built into processes of interaction functions only inasmuch as the persons involved in it acknowledge each other's role and have congruent assumptions about them.

Two more things remain to be said. First, it is obvious that this steering process is not necessarily held up until the sanctions are actually encountered. The mutual role knowledge enables the actors to calculate the consequences of their actions beforehand, so that much of the mutual steering takes place on the level of anticipations. Let us note, incidentally, that the analogy with feed-back systems still holds, now with 'anticipatory feed-backs'.[1]

Secondly, it is clear also that role behaviour is not corrected only by this mutual steering, in the course of normal role interplay. For special roles exist whose behavioural content consists mainly or even exclusively of sanctioning procedures, such as the roles of magistrates, elders, judges, parents, teachers. Here the sanction is no longer a by-product of the meeting of roles (of any kind), when actors in one role as it were run up against actors in others and the different role performances must be made to fit in with one another. Rather, the sanctions, whether corrective or reinforcing, are part of an embracing control design and a specific maintenance machinery. It is part of this design to provide a distinct class of 'authority roles', so constructed that their actors may supervise, guide, and correct the actors in all other roles. Which is a special case of that intervention by 'third parties' which we touched upon a little earlier.

[1] Norbert Wiener, *Cybernetics*, 1948, p. 133.

Let me try and apply my system of notation to this mutual steering process. In order to do this I shall argue as follows. When one person in his role (P_1) acts towards another (P_2) in a certain manner (a), this will be, for P_2, initially a 'passive' attribute, P_2 being merely 'acted towards' and noting the fact. We indicate the passive aspect by writing the symbol for this item of behaviour as a fraction ($\frac{1}{a}$). Assuming the action 'a' to be in conformity with the obtaining norms, then its active form will be appropriate to P_1's role, and its passive form, to P_2's role, each role implying ($\supset$) the respective version of 'a':

(8) $\qquad P_1 \supset P_1 (a \ldots) : P_2$
$\qquad\qquad P_2 \supset P_2 (\frac{1}{a} \ldots) : P_1$

We were assuming, further, that in such cases P_2's response will be a rewarding sanction (rs). If however P_1 acted in any other, unorthodox, fashion, i.e. in the manner 'non-a' (-a), P_2's response would be punitive (ps). Again, if both these responses are in conformity with the obtaining norms, they will be implied in both roles as the two actors see them, in active and passive form respectively. Since 'a' with its consequence 'rs', and '-a' with its consequence 'ps', are alternatives, we can write—

(9) $\qquad P_1 \supset (a \ldots \frac{1}{s})/(-a \ldots \frac{1}{ps}) : P_2$
$\qquad\qquad P_2 \supset (\frac{1}{a} \ldots rs)/(-\frac{1}{a} \ldots ps) : P_1$

The inspection of the two formulae shows them to be complementary; differently put, they illustrate a situation in which the two actors see their roles in an equivalent manner. Let us use the logical symbol $\equiv$ for 'equivalence', and translate (9) into relationship terms, in accordance with our earliest formula (1) (see p. 10 above); simplifying a little by letting 's' stand for both types of sanctioning response, we can write—

(10) $\qquad P_1 (\pm a \ldots \frac{1}{s}) : P_2 \equiv P_2 (\pm \frac{1}{a} \ldots s) : P_1$
$\qquad \therefore P_1 \, r \, P_2 \equiv P_2 \, r \, P_1$

This last formula may be said to indicate that the relationship between P_1 and P_2 'looks the same' from each actor's standpoint. The formula thus symbolizes that congruence of role con-

CONFORMITY AND DEVIANCE

ceptions, and the consequent equivalence of the relationships involved, which is the basic condition of the mutual steering process. If there is no such congruence, if P_1 sees his own role as excluding the sanctioning responses which P_2 sees as part of his role, then—

(11) $\quad P_1 \supset P_1 (\pm a \ldots - \frac{1}{s}) : P_2$
$\qquad P_2 \supset P_2 (\pm \frac{1}{a} \ldots s) : P_1$
$\qquad P_1 (\pm a \ldots - \frac{1}{s}) : P_2 \not\equiv P_2 (\pm \frac{1}{a} \ldots s) : P_1$
$\therefore P_1 \, r \, P_2 \not\equiv P_2 \, r \, P_1$

Formula (11), then, stands for incongruent role conceptions and for relationships which no longer 'look the same' from each actor's standpoint, its two forms ceasing to be complementary or equivalent. It is clear that such relationships must involve incompatibility and conflict.

Let me break off at this point and make this comment only. As we have been using our symbols and formulae, they have gone some way beyond mere attempts at notation; for their inspection and manipulation proved capable of leading to novel and empirically relevant conclusions. In other words, our notational system approximates to a *calculus*. Though as yet it does no more, it proves, I think, in this crucial respect its value as an analytical tool.

3

The main conclusion to be drawn from the preceding discussion concerns the complementariness of role conceptions or expectations. More precisely, we established that the roles linked in the mutual steering process *posit* or *implicate* one another; for if

$$P_1 \supset (a \ldots \tfrac{1}{s})$$

there must be a P_2 such that

(12) $\qquad P_2 \supset (\tfrac{1}{a} \ldots s)$

$\therefore P_1 \supset P_2$ and *vice versa*

This conclusion can be stated in more general terms. For it is true of any role or quasi-role (since it always 'materializes in an interaction context') that it must implicate others, the behaviour implicit in one role always having some reference to or being in some measure determined by the behaviour implicit in others. We should, however, distinguish two aspects or degrees of this mutual implication. The first is of the interactive type just discussed, when roles are designed to meet in direct interplay, each role having a given efficiency (or responsiveness) *vis-à-vis* another. The second aspect is primarily distributive and only indirectly interactive, representing the corollary of the basic fact about all roles, that they are differential modes of behaviour.

So understood, the mutual implication of roles merely signifies (loosely speaking) the obtaining 'division of labour'. More precisely, it signifies that each actor in his role knows about all the other roles from which his own differs in some manner, and is guided by this knowledge in his own actions. We might say he carries a role map of his society in his head, indicating the way in which his role fits in amongst others. This map need only be a rough one, though one sufficiently accurate to show the boundaries between any actor's role and relevant others—similar, as it were adjacent, roles or perhaps opposed ones. So that a 'father' will act in full knowledge of how his position compares with that of an 'uncle' or 'teacher'; a 'doctor', of how his right to the confidences of his patients compares with that of a 'friend' or 'priest'; and so forth.

The map which people carry in their heads may be less than rough and approximate; where the general consensus on the proper character of roles is weak, the maps of different people will altogether fail to tally and to add up to a uniform, unambiguous total map. This kind of subjectivity seems typical of the class conceptions current in modern society. The fluidity of judgments about one's own and other people's class position is amply evidenced in recent literature, which indeed tends to call in question the whole 'objectivity' of social classes and their existence as tangible, 'discrete social units'.[1] We need say no

[1] See John F. Cuber and William F. Kenkel, *Social Stratification in the United States*, 1954, p. 307.

more on this large subject save repeat that the perception of class membership and all that it entails in the way of differential conduct, privileges and 'disprivileges', is always a significant item on those 'distributive maps', however indefinite their design.

We can relate them, further, to the fashionable concept of 'reference groups', much used in contemporary sociology and social psychology, though its somewhat confused meaning would need to be clarified and possibly corrected.[1] Even the name is misleading since, in practice, it often signifies a 'social category', a class of people, 'rather than an actual group'.[2] Often, too, the sheer cognitive process involved in the 'reference' (to a particular group or class of people) is confused with 'identification' or 'allegiance'; or it is given another, even heavier, emotional weighting, bearing on the sense of deprivation, gratification, or ambition with which people tend to perceive their own position relative to that of others. But 'reference group' can, perhaps profitably, be emptied of all these secondary implications. It then becomes a purely 'differentiational' category and one that is, in principle, 'emotionally neutral'.[3] Like our distributive map it merely indicates that people of a particular description (or role) will appraise their own situation and conduct in the light of their knowledge of other classes of people with whom they compare themselves (or whom they make their point of 'reference').

It is difficult, and would be clumsy, always to keep distinct these two aspects of the mutual implication of roles, one interactive, the other distributive. Nor is it relevant in the present context. Understood in either sense the mutual implication of roles entitles us to regard, with Talcott Parsons, the role inventory of any society as a role *system*. But by 'system' I mean no more than an array of elements which are 'compatible' and so constituted that 'all elements are determined by some at least of the other elements'.[4] For even a cursory inspection will show

[1] See Theodore M. Newcomb, in *For a Science of Social Man*, ed. John Gillin, pp. 242-3.
[2] Elizabeth Bott, 'The Concept of Class as a Reference Group', *Human Relations*, vol. vii, 1954, p. 266.
[3] Elizabeth Bott, op. cit. p. 264.
[4] S. Stebbing, *A Modern Introduction to Logic*, p. 196.

that the role system is no more exacting or pervasive than that; in other words, it is not a 'coherent system' (in Stebbing's sense) that is, one in which the mutual determination of 'elements' is complete, every role being related to every other role.

In the discussion that follows I propose to concern myself further with the mutual implications of roles, the system they constitute, and the limits set to its 'coherence'. Now all this can be expressed in different terms. Since the mutual implication of roles means that the behaviour incumbent upon the actor in any one role always bears a reference to the behaviour of other actors in their roles, it also means that the respective actors stand in definable relationships to one another. And inasmuch as the roles existing in any society combine to form a system, in virtue of the actor relationships, they also build up that ordered, overall arrangement which we have decided to call a social structure. Here, then, the present discussion links up with the earlier stages of our enquiry. Everything that we shall now have to say about the way roles implicate one another (or fail to do so) will serve to demonstrate the kind of 'social structure' we can hope to extract from or define for concrete societies.

4

It is purely a matter of convenience that I shall proceed as though the 'extraction' of a social structure presupposed the prior compilation of a role inventory. This is obviously not the case. Precisely because roles implicate one another, the description or analysis of any set of roles already includes the analysis of the relationships between them, and hence of sectors of the 'social structure' as here understood. Differently put, the analysis of roles and of the social structure will tend to proceed *pari passu*, though the full 'extraction' of the latter may well involve an additional reordering of the material and special problems of presentation. Occasionally anthropologists have chosen a method of presentation whereby they single out particular roles and outline social structure on this basis, reaching it by way of a role inventory (or a section of it).[1] Usually, we describe roles as

[1] Cf. the treatment of certain kinship roles in Eggan's study of the Hopi (*Social Organization of the Western Pueblos*) and in Fortes's *The Web of Kinship among the Tallensi*.

they become relevant and as we proceed with the general analysis. Needless to say, this is also how we investigate them; no one would think of preparing a role inventory first, as a preliminary step before embarking on the study of relationships or whatever else a 'structural' analysis entails.

Nor would this be feasible, for there is no ready way to define or be sure about the limits of any role inventory. Roles, as we recall, are refined from that ubiquitous raw material—names for types or classes of people. But this preliminary linguistic evidence is subject to considerable correction; and the correction may well include the addition of roles construed by the observer. This complication apart, we cannot even indicate beforehand the potential maximum of any role inventory, save very roughly. Very roughly, it lies in the total vocabulary current in any given society and expressing its notions about differences of persons. The approximate nature of this clue is perhaps best exemplified by classificatory kinship terminologies. The names embracing a number of biologically distinct kinship degrees strongly suggest a corresponding coincidence or reduction of kinship roles; yet, as is well known, the persons all called 'father' or 'brother', or whatever the case may be, may well be differentiated by their respective rights and obligations towards ego, to a degree conceivably amounting to differences in roles proper. Conversely, kinsfolk differently named may yet be alike in their playing of roles. More generally speaking, actual usage would have to corroborate our assumptions about the potential maximum of role inventories; and each named identity and difference would have to be tested for its true role character, in the manner previously discussed. Again, I cannot imagine anyone proceeding in this way. Above all, as we know, ambiguities would still remain, so that no role inventory can ever be really clear-cut or final.

Even so, to gain some notion of the order of magnitude involved in the role inventories of primitive societies, I have attempted to estimate the number of different roles existing in certain comparable communities—the ten Nuba tribes described in my monograph. I divided the roles according to sex, the female roles proving invariably less numerous than the male ones. A few roles (never less than three, never more than five) applied to both sexes indiscriminately. The proportion, incidentally, of kinship roles in the total number varied between one-half and one-third. The sexually differentiated roles fell within the ranges 25-43 for males (M) and 16-33 for females (F), with this incidence among the 10 tribes:

Range of Roles	Number of Tribes Sharing the Range	
	M.	F.
15-19	—	3
20-24	—	5
25-29	4	1
30-34	4	1
35-39	1	—
40-44	1	—

Rough and imprecise though this estimate may be, it is interesting in that it shows a fair measure of agreement or at least not too irregular a scatter. But beyond this very general comment I will not go.

If we cannot compile really complete and precise role inventories, cannot we at least produce a comprehensive classification of roles, devise appropriate categories and, on that basis, draw up something like a logical chart into which all role inventories must fit? Our empirical knowledge of roles seems wide enough for this. Yet no systematic attempts of this kind exist, though Talcott Parsons and Marion J. Levy have defined certain basic categories. As an experiment, I have tried to work out such a taxonomy of roles (see p. 53): the criteria underlying it have to some extent been introduced already; others will become clear later. Again, I shall present the results without further comment. I would only emphasize two things. The categorization of roles is based mainly on their content, i.e. on the particular conduct they are meant to imply; it does not take into account the internal structure of roles—their being 'focused' or 'non-focused', 'triggered-off' or 'unfolding'. Furthermore, the 'role chart' is not only tentative but also very broadly conceived, including only major categories and making no reference to the possibility of classifying certain roles in alternative ways.

IV

THE COHERENCE OF ROLE SYSTEMS

IN this section we shall mainly be concerned with the interconnection of roles and with the coherence of the role system (or 'social structure') that thus emerges. First, however, I propose to consider a very special type of interconnection, presupposed in the subsequent discussion, namely the interconnection, or *summation*, of roles played by identical actors.

It is a sociological truism that every individual fills several roles both successively in his lifetime and simultaneously at any given time. The *modus operandi* of this succession and coincidence of roles presents no new problem, both being engineered by the usual mechanisms of recruitment. All that is new is that the preconditions for the assumption of additional roles now include not only ordinary, as it were autonomous, human attributes, but attributes indicating the performance (perhaps the successful performance) of specified other roles, previously or concurrently. Examples are of course familiar—political posts open only to 'family heads' or 'men of the people'; a husband automatically becoming a 'son-in-law'; a great 'scholar' or a 'philanthropist' qualifying for positions of social prominence, and so forth.

The ambiguity entailed in the definition of certain roles occurs again on this level; it now concerns the difficulty of separating the linked roles played by the same individual from a single role series. The primary evidence for the presence of the former is again linguistic: it is simply a fact that an 'old man' will be called such in certain situations, while in others he will be referred to, say, as a 'wise man', or that a man will be known as a 'husband' in respect of certain rights and obligations and as a 'son-in-law' in respect of others. No ambiguity arises if the linkage of roles is variable and not exclusive to the roles in question, for example, if some (not all) 'old men' are also considered 'wise', and some 'young men' equally qualify for this description. But where the roles (or presumed roles) appear in linkages which have some degree of regularity and exclusiveness, e.g. where all or most old men are considered wise and no young man ever is, we may be in doubt whether we are in fact dealing with genuinely separate roles or only with additional attributes to a given role series. Symbolically expressed, though it may appear as if a person P enacted two roles, A and B, such that

(13) $\qquad$ P (A + B), when
$\qquad\qquad\qquad$ A $\supset$ a, b, c ... n and
$\qquad\qquad\qquad$ B $\supset$ n,

in effect he might enact only one expanded role (A *or* B), such that

(14) $\qquad\qquad$ A/B = Σ a, b, c ... n

Take these further examples: Since any married man will have to assume, say, the current taboos towards his wife's mother, should we not include these among the attributes of 'husband' rather than say of him that he is assuming the additional role of 'son-in-law'? Again, if in a society (like Nupe) all women traders are expected to be also prostitutes, and *vice versa*, is this a summation of two separate roles or only the full description of one? And if the typical 'businessman' is the sort of person likely to belong to the Rotary Club and similar associations, does this indicate a probable linkage between several roles or does it only characterize the one role 'businessman'?

There is no categorical answer to such questions. This is all a matter of viewpoint and heuristic usefulness. To quote from Sprott: 'How far one says (of a person) that he is playing a multiple role, or a single one at any given moment, will depend on the purpose of one's enquiry'.[1] But we can be a little more precise; for in choosing between the two manners of description we are likely to consider two things. First, we cannot fail to consider the existing linguistic convention and the expediency of departing from it, e.g. by denying that 'son-in-law' or 'prostitute' is a separate role. More generally speaking, it will always be inexpedient to enlarge any role series so much that the role

[1] W. J. H. Sprott, *Social Psychology*, 1952, p. 154.

name ('husband', 'woman trader', 'businessman') ceases to be informative. Secondly and more importantly, we shall always consider also the compatibility of the linked series of attributes. If, for example, in a society with unilinear descent the woman as a 'wife' must give all her loyalties to her husband and his kin (lineage, clan), but as a 'daughter' or 'sister' to her own kin, it seems logical to allocate the two potentially conflicting sets of obligations to separate roles. I said 'logical' because our conception of roles, as series of interconnected ways of acting laid down by the rules of society, carries the implication that the series is always a compatible one. If then, we meet with a conflict of norms in the total behaviour of an individual, we shall tend to see it as a conflict between the roles he is made to assume rather than within any one role.

But it is not a manner of great moment whether we decide one way or the other; our analysis will in any event lead us to all the attributes making up the presumed role or combination of roles. I shall, therefore, in the following largely disregard this possible ambiguity. Nor can I attach much importance to the question what we should call the summation of all the roles individuals might be expected to play: 'General Role', 'Role Personality', or 'Social Personality' are three names which have been proposed. These names actually suggest more than a mere summation, namely a merging or integration of all roles in some sort of super-role. This seems to me a dubious assumption; I frankly cannot picture the concrete case. Indeed, I would suggest that closer analysis will always show the alleged super-role to be in effect only one of the several roles enacted by an individual, selected because it appears to be the one most powerful in his life or the one most consequential considering the general character of the society: which condition is most frequently satisfied by occupational roles ('he is a teacher through and through', 'he is a soldier first and foremost'), and roles indicating economic standing and civil status ('socio-economic status', as one often says). To some extent, then, the presumed super-role may prove to indicate no more than the 'halo effect' discussed earlier.

There seems to be an exception, however. In primitive societies the linkage of roles may be so firm and predictable that individuals do appear to act in such embracing, overall roles. Simplifying a little we can visualize a situation where a 'father' is always the head of a household, the teacher of his children, the 'manager' of a labour team, a 'councillor' or 'elder' of the community, an officiant in rituals, and one of the 'onlookers' in dances or sports; while a 'son' will always be a subordinate member of the household, a 'pupil' or 'trainee', a 'worker' in the labour team, a 'common citizen', one of the congregation in rituals, and an active participant in dances and sports. (Similar linkages can of course be established for other roles—'grandfathers', 'married women', etc.). Since in such combinations it is, for obvious reasons, the contingent condition (being a father or son) which determines the assumption of all the concomitant roles, the description of a man as a 'father' or 'son' will in fact amount to describing almost his complete social being (or 'personality'). But this is simply the possibility mentioned before, when the series of firmly linked roles might equally be regarded as a single, more broadly conceived role, extended by the inclusion of additional attributes. And whether we speak of summation or extension, it still is a process of combination and linkage in which the components can be isolated.

The combination as such, however, is important also from another point of view. One of the consequences of this process must be the reduction in the number of genuinely separate or separable roles in the society. And since each role involves its actor in appropriate relationships with actors in other roles, the reduced separability of roles also entails a reduced separability of relationships. The 'family head' who is also a 'manager', 'priest', and 'elder' will thus be linked with persons who are at once 'kinsfolk' or 'dependents', 'workers', members of the 'congregation,' and 'common citizens', in this fourfold manner. Differently expressed, a series of diverse relationships (domestic or kin, economic, religious, political) will come to link the same sets of persons, constituting a congruent set of linkages. Which means that the society is to that extent rendered less complex and more homogeneous.

This multiplication of relationships stretching between the same actors has been recognized by several scholars as a characteristic feature of primitive societies. Firth and others speak of the 'many-stranded quality of relationships'[1]: this is a slightly misleading description since it suggests single relationships of a complex order rather than a bundle or set of congruent relationships. Perhaps we might, more accurately, speak of a *manifold* of relationships. The lesser complexity of a society operating with such relationship manifolds has equally been pointed out. Gluckman suggests that a social structure in which there is a high degree of 'congruence in the links between . . . persons' should be called a relatively 'uncomplicated' structure; a society in which links are not congruent, tending to relate any given person 'with many different persons in various systems of ties', is by contrast a 'complicated' structure.[2]

Once more, the choice of names is not altogether a happy one. For the term 'uncomplicated' obscures the distinction between sheer quantitative simplicity and the reduced complexity we have in mind, which is the result of rules of combination. A society differentiating between four pairs of roles, say, family head and dependent, manager and worker, elder and common citizen, priest and worshipper, is undoubtedly more complex or complicated than one acknowledging two only, e.g. having no 'managers' (because each man works on his own) and no 'priests' (because all worship is strictly communal). Needless to say the relationships involved are similarly reduced in number, the 'simpler' society lacking two relationships present in the more 'complex' one (manager-workers, priest-congregation). But think now of a society which, while exhibiting the same fourfold (or eightfold) differentiation of roles and relationships, combines the actors, in one of these ways:

(a) Family head   = manager
    dependent   = worker
    elder   = priest
    common citizen = worshipper;

(b) Family head = manager = elder = priest
    Dependent = worker = common citizen = worshipper.

This is clearly an altogether different type of non-complexity.

[1] Raymond Firth, 'Social Anthropology', *Encyclopaedia Britannica*, 1955 ed., p. 863.
[2] Max Gluckman, *The Judicial Process among the Barotse of Northern Rhodesia*, pp. 19-20.

The possible relationships, like the roles on which they hinge, are not reduced in number but, as it were, in their scatter through the population. Thus, the social system is not simply less 'complicated' (indeed, the component relationship manifolds might be said to make it more so): perhaps it might be called more highly *combinative* or *involute*.

There is, admittedly, the more familiar and less far-fetched term 'homogeneous', which may serve as well. Fortes recently pointed out that 'just what we mean by a homogeneous society is still rather vague though we all use the term lavishly'.[1] If we adopt it to indicate the character of such 'combinative' or 'involute' systems we shall at the same time improve the precision of the term; for the scale and regularity of the summation of roles (and of the attendant multiplication of relationships) seems to provide the needed criterion for the definition, and probably the measurement, of this crucial yet elusive phenomenon.

Now Fortes's own 'working definition' of social homogeneity is this: A homogeneous society is ideally one in which any person (meaning here an individual with his 'assemblage of statuses') can be substituted for any other person of the same category without bringing about changes in the social structure. This implies that any two persons of the same category have the same body of customary usages and beliefs. The paradigm of 'sibling equivalence' further suggests that such persons are 'equivalent' in regard to their 'achievable life histories'. If I understand Fortes correctly, his principle of 'social substitutability' follows from my thesis concerning the summation of roles, so that social homogeneity as he uses the term does in fact describe our 'involute' social system; and the issues involved seem sufficiently important to warrant fuller exposition.

I assume that when Fortes speaks of persons 'of the same category' being 'substituted' for one another he means something very simple—the kind of situation in which the heir or successor to any office, role or 'status' steps into the place of the previous incumbent. I assume, further, that by 'changes in the social

[1] 'The Structure of Unilineal Descent Groups', *American Anthropologist*, vol. 55, 1953, p. 36.

structure' Fortes means the rearrangement, possibly the dislocation, of the pre-existing ordering of relationships and roles (or 'statuses'). Picture, then, the replacement of a family head in a society where this role is firmly combined with those of elder and priest: the successor to the headship of the family will then automatically assume the other two offices as well. As a result, all the roles will be kept in being; furthermore, the relationships which used to link the family head-cum-elder-cum-priest with others will be preserved, with their given pattern and degree of congruence. Consider now the opposite case—a society where the three roles are not firmly interconnected, being only fortuitously combined in the person of a particular family head. On his replacement a number of changes are apt to happen: one or the other concomitant role may disappear, at least temporarily, until a separate, new actor is recruited; or the roles, though not disappearing, will be redistributed, so that the former congruence no longer holds; or finally, the successor may bring with him some new role (say, that of a leader in warfare or dancing), not formerly linked with that of family head, again disturbing the previous pattern of roles and relationships.

In the first type of society it is therefore true to say that the two persons in the same category (of family head) will ideally have the same 'achievable life histories'; equally, their substitution for one another will cause no 'changes in the social structure' (though 'shifts' is probably a better word to describe the rearrangements in question). In the second type of society, both effects are likely to be reversed. Our general conclusion, then, is that a society is 'homogeneous', providing for this substitutability of persons, to the extent to which the summation of roles current in the society is both firm and extensive, so that the summation is indeed a measure of homogeneity: which is what we set out to show.

We might add, by way of a footnote, that the summation of roles and the consequent involution of relationships are likely to occur on any significant scale only in the case of roles belonging to different sectors or areas of social life—economic, political, religious, etc. Any considerable summation of roles in the same sector would defeat the very principles of role allocation and differentiation, that is, the reason for having roles at all; while the attendant relationships might cease to be compatible or indeed workable. I am not at the moment considering the logical impossibility of conceiving of certain roles as combinable, when they represent mutually exclusive categorizations (e.g. priest and layman, a man's father and son). I am thinking of the purely practical difficulties that would arise if the 'manager' of a team also played the part of an ordinary worker in it, an 'elder' that of a common citizen, and *vice versa*. The sector of kinship is in some respects an exception since here all roles are widely combinable. Obviously, anyone is likely to be, at the same time, a father, son, brother, husband, uncle, cousin. Equally obviously, he is so to different persons; that is to say, there is no corresponding congruence and involution of relationships. Preferential marriage rules, e.g. of cross-cousin marriage, do bring about a certain measure of congruence (spouses being also cousins, a mother's brother a father-in-law, a father's sister a mother-in-law). But other marriage rules, in the form of incest taboos and rules of exogamy, on the contrary restrict any such coincidence of ties, and hence the risk of creating unworkable combinations of relationships. It is worth keeping this in mind when discussing the 'many-strandedness' of relationships in primitive societies; for however 'involute' they may prove to be in other respects, in the sector of kinship they retain a maximum of 'scatter' and separability.

This seems the appropriate place to consider briefly the advantages and disadvantages of the summation of roles, judged from the viewpoint of the society engineering it. As regards the disadvantages, we have already suggested the main danger: it is that of imposing upon individuals roles and relationships which are incompatible, and hence creating strains and tensions both in the personality and in the society itself. I have quoted earlier the example of the conflict of loyalties facing any woman who is a 'wife', 'sister', and 'daughter' at the same time (see p. 65). It has its corollary in the strained relations between a man and his wife's kin, who are in a sense strangers to one another and hence potentially hostile, yet must live amicably together; and there is no need for further illustrations. Societies have evolved various devices and conventions, more or less successful, meant to resolve these difficulties. One, for example, is the formal dissociation of the roles and relationships in conflict, as when the wife is explicitly adopted into the husband's kin or lineage (and hence ceases to be a 'sister' or 'daughter'); another, the creation or recognition of intermediary roles (such as the 'clanswoman' among the Tallensi, who is understood to stand halfway between her natal clan and that of her husband).[1] The joking relationships so-called, in Radcliffe-Brown's classical interpretation, offer a third solution, now through conventionalizing a sham hostility between relatives by marriage, at which no offence is taken, so that it reconciles 'the separateness of the two groups . . . with the need of maintaining friendly relations'.[2] Where such conventions are lacking or prove unsuccessful the disturbing psychological effects of the incompatibility of roles remain unchecked. Students of personality are well aware of this possibility; indeed, 'some psychiatrists have speculated that neurosis often arises from the individual's demand for consistency in his behaviour in all roles'.[3]

The advantages of role summation lie in the strengthening of social integration and of social control. For the more roles an individual combines in his person, the more is he linked by relationships with persons in other roles and in diverse areas of social life. Equally, any additional role assumed by an individual ties him more firmly to the norms of his society. Our examples of a 'family head' (or a successful family head) attaining political office and a 'philanthropist' social prominence, illustrate this point; for if it is desirable to achieve such prominence, this motivation will dictate those other interests, to make a success of the headship of families or to engage in philanthropy. If this involves the idea of a reward or 'premium', the opposite effect is that of 'penalization', when the failure to perform a certain role according to the norms or ideals of the society entails unsuccess in attaining another, valued, role. More generally speaking, role overlaps can function as 'linked incentives' so that, through their linkage, the normative behaviour

---

[1] See M. Fortes, *The Dynamics of Clanship among the Tallensi*, 1945, chap. IX.
[2] See *African Systems of Kinship and Marriage*, p. 57.
[3] Kluckhohn and Murray, *Personality in Nature, Society and Culture*, p. 268.

implicit in one role is safeguarded by the value character of the other.[1]

Why should there be a summation of roles at all? I do not quite know how to answer this since we simply cannot conceive of a society entirely without it. But this much can, I think, safely be said. The summation of roles is an aspect of the general principle of 'allocation' which we discussed before; it forms part of the basic 'economy' of societies, in the sense that it reflects the balance between needs (to have such-and-such proficiencies, interests and aims represented in the population) and resources (the human beings available).

2

We now return to our main problem, the coherence of role systems. The simplest way to approach it is by means of a small-scale model of a (fictitious) role inventory. The table on p. 73 represents such a model, a miniature role system as it were. Though fictitious, it contains roles familiar and widely current in primitive societies, though obviously it does not contain them all. The table is arranged in conformity with my logical 'role chart', (see p. 53) in such a fashion that the rows contain logically related roles, and each row corresponds to one of the logical categories into which roles can be grouped; these are indicated by the numbers on the right. Presenting the roles in this abstract fashion, not based on information referring to some particular society, we cannot avoid certain ambiguities of classification. This is true, for example, of 'leadership roles' (row B) and 'expressive roles' (row C), which might in certain societies be such as to warrant their inclusion in 'occupational roles' (row D); again, varying with the circumstances, a role like 'priest' might belong to any of these three categories, and certain 'status roles' (row A) might coincide with 'leadership roles'. The fact that there are three columns has no further significance; in certain cases the number of horizontal cells could be greatly extended, while in others it would fall short of three. The blank spaces in one of the rows will be explained presently.

[1] See S. F. Nadel, 'Social Control and Self-Regulation', *Social Forces*, 1953, vol. 31, p. 268.

MINIATURE ROLE SYSTEM

A	noble	commoner	slave	(7)
B	chief	priest	elder	(7)
C	poet	musician		(4)
D	merchant	doctor	blacksmith	(5)
E	old man	youth	child	(1)
F	pagan	Moslem	Christian	(4)
G	native	stranger		(1)
H		able-bodied	cripple	(1)
I	brave	coward		(1)
J {				(1)(2)
	father	sister's son	wife	
K	patron	client		(7)
L		friend		(6)
M		blood-brother		(6)

The first thing to be noted is that roles in different rows (ignoring ambiguities of classification) do not lend themselves to interrelation. It simply makes no sense to construe any 'mutual implications', viz. actor relationships, between such roles as chief, father, pagan, old man, friend, coward, musician. This is clearly a consequence of the diverse or, more precisely, disparate logical basis of these categorizations. And it is simply an empirical fact, which need not be explored further, that all role systems similarly include numerous logical cleavages, that is, are constructed with the aid of disparate *differentiae*. We might, perhaps, point out that this follows from the class character of roles; for class concepts in general may be equally disparate, as the standard examples in any text book on Logic will show. Since logicians often take their illustrations from their own society they also illustrate to that extent the disparity of roles (or of potential roles), as in this example: 'bad-tempered individuals, professors, women, locomotive engineers'.[1] Now whenever a categorization of items, of whatever kind, is constructed in this disparate fashion, the resulting classes are apt to be mutually inclusive, wholly or partially. This is again true of roles. The corollary of the logical cleavage of roles, then, is the fact that any two roles belonging to different logical categories may be found represented by the same actors. Which underlines the impossibility of speaking of the part played by a 'chief' *vis-à-vis* a 'father', a 'pagan' *vis-à-vis* an 'old man', a 'friend' *vis-à-vis* a 'coward', or a 'musician' *vis-à-vis a* 'cripple', simply because the same person may be an actor in each of these paired roles.

I shall call the logical categories or classes of roles *role frames* for short. Let us be clear that they do not necessarily coincide with the sets of roles belonging to different areas of social life (economic, political, etc.) and distinguished by the quality of the particular interests they subserve. The truth of this can at once be seen. Two roles, for example, both belonging to the area of kinship, 'family head' and 'father', or two 'religious' roles like 'priest' and 'believer', are yet logically disparate, being based on different principles of categorization; while roles

[1] This example is taken from Cohen and Nagel, *An Introduction to Logic and Scientific Method*, 1947, pp. 14-15.

belonging to different areas may be logically related, e.g. when they all refer to occupations (judge, merchant, clergyman).

The examples quoted before, illustrating the mutual inclusiveness of disparate roles probably carry sufficient conviction. Admittedly, not all examples we can think of would sound as convincing, mainly because we might have empirical knowledge of societies where the logically disparate roles are *in fact* mutually exclusive, e.g. when a 'slave' cannot be a 'merchant', a 'chief' not a 'pagan', a 'priest' not a 'husband' or a 'wife' not a 'stranger'. In such societies the fuller analysis of the roles would then demonstrate the relevant recruitment principle, that is, the restrictions which make the disparate roles mutually exclusive and hence capable of interrelation.

Whether or not they are so interrelated of course depends entirely on the concrete social situation and is to that extent a fortuitous matter. By their character, the roles do in no way implicate other, counterpart roles, and thus bridge the logical cleavage. But there are three further, true, exceptions of the role of logical cleavages—'true' in the sense that here the logical cleavage is overruled by a regular interrelation, required by the character of certain roles and valid wherever these occur.

(1) The first exception concerns *leadership* or *authority roles*, which always imply, as part of the influence vested in them, the supervision of all or numerous other roles in the society, disparity and mutual inclusiveness notwithstanding. The logical cleavages will simply be regarded as irrelevant; that is, it will tacitly be assumed that, say, a 'chief' has to concern himself with the conduct of 'fathers' or 'Moslems' and to act towards them in a determinate manner, and that he would do so in his official capacity regardless of the fact that he may himself be a 'father' or 'Moslem'.

(2) Our second exception are *expressive roles*. The name is meant to indicate that there the actors' task is the communication of ideas and emotional experiences through manipulating, applying, and perhaps creatively adding to the expressive symbols current in the society.[1] Actors in these roles, therefore, are likely to be concerned with topics bearing on the character and

[1] Cf. Talcott Parsons, *The Social System*, p. 409.

conduct of all or numerous other roles. Thus a 'priest' might make pronouncements upon marriage and hence upon the position of 'husbands,' or upon the obedience of 'sons' to 'fathers'; a poet might eulogize youth, heroes, lovers, friends, and so forth. Again, we tacitly disregard the possibility of the priest or poet being himself all these other things, and consider only their determinate manner of acting in regard to actors in the other roles.

(3) The final exception concerns roles which imply the rendering of *services* to others, and involve that kind of contractual relationship. I am using 'services' in the strictly economic sense of the word, meaning an 'output' capable of satisfying wants or needs, the two meeting in some sort of 'open market'. Occupational roles and to some extent expressive roles (in so far as they are 'commercialized') are paradigms. Thus a carpenter might make chairs and tables for people who need them, whoever they may be; a doctor is similarly expected to treat all and sundry; and a poet will compose poems meant to appeal to everybody, of whatever description. We note that this service relationship does not predicate any link between two sets of specific roles, but only a link between one specific role and an anonymous 'public' embracing many, perhaps all other roles, that is, the rest of the society. Often, however, the anonymous public is narrowed down and differentiated in role terms, in one of two ways. Either the 'market' specifies a particular section of the population, in terms of pre-existing roles, as when a court poet or musician performs only for the nobility, a medical practitioner is a 'poor man's doctor', or a 'priest' never officiates for strangers. Or the public, the recipients of the services, upon entering into the contractual relationship will also assume a particular role or quasi-role, more or less enduring or sharply defined; in this sense the public of a craftsman become his 'customers' or 'patrons', the public of a doctor his 'patients', and that of poets and priests, an 'audience' or 'congregation'. This narrowing-down of an anonymous public involves a process akin to *personalization;* more precisely, it indicates the degree to which such one-versus-all relationships become personalized, as it were at the receiving end.

Now in all cases not covered by our exceptions, we are left with heterogeneous role frames without a common logical locus, incapable of interrelation, and thus incapable of yielding a coherent, embracing structure. At least, this is so if we equate 'interrelation' with actor relationships, resting on the behaviour of individuals *vis-à-vis* one another. Sometimes we can construe distributive interrelations, suggestive of a division of labour (see pp. 76, 78), where actor relationships proper are precluded. This happens when the disparate roles have some attribute or function in common in virtue of which they become logically akin and comparable. (Also, the context would make it clear that we are considering roles filled by different persons). It is thus that we could previously compare 'fathers' and 'teachers', since both deal with children, or 'doctors', 'priests', and 'friends', since all three act as confidants. But ignoring this unimportant exception, the only kind of interrelation between disparate roles which can be construed would have to be framed in altogether different terms, namely, in the terms of their mutual inclusiveness and of the recruitment roles laying down the extent and manner in which actors in one role will also assume or change to other roles. Thus, though 'family head' and 'priest' remain disparate roles, if any man who is a family head is also, or is likely to become, a priest, the two roles can yet be interrelated, in this other manner.

This is clearly a substitute solution. In a sense, we are making a virtue out of a necessity, using the very fact which vitiates the construction of actor relationships for the construction of interrelations based on recruitment. But the latter have a significance of their own. In so far as they rest on firm rules regulating the flow of the population into given roles and combinations of roles they do indicate the sort of thing we are after—a type of 'orderliness'. It has to do with the allocation of human material to roles rather than with role behaviour itself: even so, it stands for a system, for a coherent alignment or arrangement. Its importance in primitive, 'homogeneous' societies, where numerous roles are thus firmly combined, need not be especially emphasized.

And this has a wider application. Since the interrelations through recruitment offer a way to link disparate role frames, and since roles within these frames do involve actor relationships proper, the recruitment rules offer a way also to interrelate relationships. The interrelation now refers to the possible overlap or coincidence of the human material in diverse relationships. For example, if the disparate roles 'family head' and 'priest' can be related on the grounds of their mutual inclusiveness, the relationships between a family head and his kinsfolk on one side, and between a priest and his congregation on the other, can be interrelated in the same fashion; which means that it becomes possible to define how far and in what manner kinship relationships and ritual relationships coincide or interpenetrate. Furthermore, it is only a short step from this linkage of relationships to the same kind of linkage between whole 'areas of relationships', that is, sub-groups, e.g. kin groups at large and congregations at large. Once more it will be a linkage resting on coincidence and interpenetration—now concerning the personnel of sub-groups and similar subdivisions of society.

I have elsewhere listed the main types of sub-groups as defined by the presence or absence of this interpenetration: sub-groups overlapping in their personnel, fortuitously or by planned coincidence; 'sections', which are mutually exclusive subdivisions of the society without being exhaustive ones; and 'segments' which are both.[1] But this is a static description, of states of affairs as they obtain at a given point of time. We could analyse them further, from a dynamic point of view, considering the processes of interpenetration rather than their end results.

We could point out, for example, that certain sub-groups (in the first category) function so-to-speak as 'feeder groups', feeding people into other groups or into the society at large. The family does so in a very basic sense, literally creating the individuals who will afterwards assume group memberships, roles and relationships of all kinds. Other feeder groups function as interim stages in the life history of individuals (age grades, schools, etc.), preparing them for the subsequent move to other, possibly terminal, groups. In either case the feeder group may retain its hold over the individuals, completely, as in the family, or partially and tenuously, as in those transitory groups. In either case too, the feeder group and the recipient group represent unlike and conceivably disparate social units. But the

[1] See my *Foundations*, pp. 176-8.

feeding-in of personnel also occurs between like and repetitive units (clans and lineages, social strata, occupational groups) and thus between sections or segments in the sense defined above; which means that the individuals will be expected to shed their original identity more or less successfully when moving from one of these mutually exclusive subdivisions to another. I take it that the concept of *circulation*, as in the 'circulation of élites' (Pareto) or 'circulation of women' (Lévi-Strauss), refers to this particular process.

Once more, the interrelations by recruitment, viewed as part of a 'feeder system', form something in the nature of a 'coherent alignment' and present an instance—a first instance—of that overall orderliness which we have made the object of this whole enquiry. But since they refer to recruitment, to the allocation of people to roles, relationships and groups, they belong only to the distributive aspect or level of social structure. In a sense, they do not even belong to that; for what is being distributed is not roles, relationships or groups, but only the population filling them. It is true that the flow or circulation of people will often imply the existence of like and repetitive social units (exogamous clans, endogamous castes, social strata with a given mobility), that is, it will take place within a clear-cut distributive pattern (see p. 17). Even so, the recruitment rules only provide the mechanics which make the pattern possible. Let me put it this way: in constructing interrelations based on recruitment we are still at the threshold of social structure: we are dealing with the technical or organizational prerequisites of orderliness rather than with social orderliness itself.

3

To turn to logically related roles. We shall see that they form a continuum between two extremes. One is constituted by roles in the case of which the logical relation also implies, with logical compulsion, an *actual* relationship between the respective actors. In other words, a given role is so conceived that, by its character, it requires to be enacted *vis-à-vis* another counterpart or correlative role. The second extreme is constituted by roles in the case of which the logical relation merely means that actual relationships between the actors are possible, not in any logical sense necessary. For reasons which will become clear presently I will call the first type of roles *dependent*, and the second, *independent* roles. It seems convenient to start with the latter.

(I) *Independent Roles*

I have just said that the actual relationships between actors in logically related roles are only *possible*, not necessary. Now if we look for instances to illustrate such logically possible relationships we may well find that those which do in fact occur, occur with some compulsion, being obligatory in the given society. But there is this to be noted. Both the occurrence and the required-ness of the relationship are purely empirical conditions, which can be determined only for the concrete case. Take these examples, all referring to roles within single role frames. Without knowing more about the concrete social situation we obviously cannot say whether a 'merchant' in that capacity does play a specific part *vis-à-vis* a 'doctor' or a 'labourer', though all three are occupational roles; nor can we predicate such a relationship between a 'priest', a 'poet', and a 'musician', though all three are expressive roles. Nor yet can we be certain, in spite of wide experience to the contrary, that the behaviour incumbent upon 'old men' and 'children', roles defined by the same criterion, age, is such that the rules prescribing it refer specifically to the other, opposed or complementary role. The actors in these roles do of course play some part *vis-à-vis* others; as already stated, occupational and expressive roles are indeed designed to provide particular services from which actors in other roles should benefit. But the 'other' roles need not be differentiated; rather, they may all be submerged, in the manner discussed earlier on, in a more or less anonymous 'public', ultimately in the 'rest of society'.

Thus a 'merchant' will clearly enter into relationships with his customers and suppliers, a public which may include 'doctors' and 'labourers'; a 'doctor', with his patients, who may include 'merchants', and 'labourers'; and so forth. Combining the two (often overlapping) role frames, occupational and expressive, we can represent the situation in a table, thus—

THE COHERENCE OF ROLE SYSTEMS

Priest ⟶ congregation

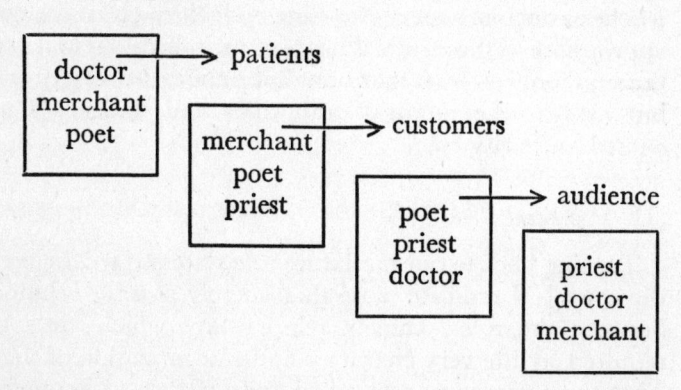

```
┌──────────┐
│ doctor   │⟶ patients
│ merchant │   ┌──────────┐
│ poet     │   │ merchant │⟶ customers
└──────────┘   │ poet     │   ┌──────────┐
               │ priest   │   │ poet     │⟶ audience
               └──────────┘   │ priest   │   ┌──────────┐
                              │ doctor   │   │ priest   │
                              └──────────┘   │ doctor   │
                                             │ merchant │
                                             └──────────┘
```

Similarly an 'old man' will behave in the given manner towards a 'public', now the society at large, which includes children, and *vice versa*. In all these examples, then, specific roles within the same role frame still remain effectively separated; in other words, the absence of a logical cleavage between roles does not preclude their empirical or *factual dissociation*.

The anonymity of relationships which goes with this dissociation, and its opposite, personalization, are clearly in considerable measure dependent on the size and complexity of the society. That 'anonymity' is more typical of societies we call advanced, and 'personalization' of societies we call primitive, has often been suggested. But let us be clear that it need not be so, if by personalization we mean no more than 'the narrowing down of an anonymous public' to persons in particular roles. For example, high specialization, which undoubtedly goes together with technological progress and other aspects of cultural advance, may involve lesser rather than greater anonymity: a doctor who is a child specialist, a 'court musician', or a shopkeeper professing to cater for 'people of taste'—all these are specialized roles which imply the reference to special classes of persons out of the relatively anonymous public of patients, an audience, or customers. Furthermore, in a somewhat different sense it fell to the modern totalitarian regimes fully to exploit the possibilities of personalization, and hence to extend the coherence of role systems. The familiar 'politization'

G

of numerous roles of the actor-public type—artists, priests, teachers, doctors—means nothing else: through it, the conduct appropriate to these roles is made to include duties and expectations not only vis-à-vis that broadest public, the society at large, but vis-à-vis the political authorities and, indeed, actors in named authority roles.

(II) *Dependent Roles*

Turning back to our miniature role system it will be seen that the rows J-M indicate more than merely possible relationships between the roles, namely relationships which are logically required by the very character and categorization of the roles. Thus there can be no role called 'patron' unless it is opposed by the correlative role 'client', and no roles such as 'friend' or 'blood brother' unless they are partnered by other 'friends' and 'blood brothers'. Societies are full of such 'relational' roles (or 'reciprocal statuses'),[1] involving relationships which are both symmetrical and asymmetrical; such are the roles of hosts and guests, leaders and followers, partners, age-mates, rivals, as well as certain roles for which our own society and role vocabulary may offer no examples.[2]

Kinship roles (row J) exemplify this linkage most sharply, each kinship role positing and implicating an appropriate correlative one. It was in order to indicate this lack of autonomy that I have left part of the row containing kinship roles blank: the blank cells must clearly be filled in with the reciprocal roles 'child', 'mother's brother', and 'husband', or at least with a reference to the person to whom one is a 'father', 'sister's son' or 'wife'.

These are in fact the only two ways of handling kinship roles in a manner appropriate to their correlative character. The second, which corresponds to the reference to ego of our conventional kinship tables, has certain practical advantages. It

[1] W. J. H. Sprott, *Social Psychology*, p. 155.
[2] E.g. the role *konyara* among the Nuba, which usually falls to two matrilineal relations of roughly equal age and opposite sex. The relationship in question involves the prohibition of intermarriage and certain mutual obligations of a ritual character (see S. F. Nadel, *The Nuba*, p. 106).

enables us to explore without restriction the relationships between any two kinship roles or degrees. For I can in every case ask: What is the relationship between a man's (or ego's) father and the man's mother's brother? or between a man's wife and his father?—and so on. The relationship thus indirectly expressed can of course usually be translated into direct and simpler reciprocal terms. Thus we shall normally describe the relationship between a man's father and the man's mother's brother as that of brothers-in-law, and the relationship between a man's wife and his father as one between daughter-in-law and father-in-law.

Now this procedure is made possible by the free and often automatic summation of kinship roles in every person. Occasionally no such translation is possible; for example, there may be no simpler and more direct way to describe the relationship between a man's father and father-in-law. If so, we should suspect that the relationship is not sufficiently distinct or important, and the respective kinship degrees not really 'roles' worth naming specifically. But the point that concerns us here is this. Once we carry out the translation into reciprocal terms and abandon the reference to ego, we abandon also the possibility of thinking of kinship roles and relationships in this unrestricted, all-round fashion. For kinship roles cannot be treated entirely independently and related at random with one another. They must either be referred to some ego and related indirectly, on the grounds of this reference; or they can be related, directly, only with their correlative roles. In the terms of our examples, it clearly makes no sense to talk about the relationship between a 'father' (any father) and a 'wife' or 'mother's brother' (any wife or mother's brother). Exactly the same is true of all other relational roles; again, no relationship can be construed between, say, 'friend' in the absolute, and 'blood brother', 'lover' or 'guest' in the absolute. In other words, roles of this kind, though they are of logically similar construction, do not constitute a role frame within which relationships can be freely predicated. Rather, they represent so-and-so many sub-systems between which there is no mutual implication; they are isolated enclaves in the general role system, and hence introduce further cleavages breaking its coherence.

4

Compared with the relational roles, which are thus incapable of independent handling and definition, all other roles can be defined relatively independently—a 'doctor' as a man practising medicine, a 'poet' as someone writing verse, a 'Moslem' as a follower of that particular creed, and an 'old man' as just that. It is unnecessary to emphasize that the definition of these roles is only *relatively* independent: as I have suggested, dependent and independent roles represent only extremes, between which all concrete roles are ranged along a continuous scale or at least one of many degrees. I need point out only three main points on this continuum.

(i) Somewhere in mid-range are the *service* and *expressive roles*, which require a 'public' more or less specified in role terms, with counterpart roles such as 'patients', 'customers', an 'audience', a 'congregation'.

(ii) The correlative aspect is weaker in *authority* or *leadership roles* since their counterpart roles may be synonymous with that widest public, the 'rest of society' (the 'subjects' of a ruler, the 'followers' of a leader).

(iii) The correlative aspect is weakest and the 'independence' of the role strongest when a role posits others only in a *distributive* sense, the character of the role merely indicating its differentiation from others. This category includes roles named on the basis of belief, ethnic origin, age, residence, personality or somatic characteristics, and similar autonomous *differentiae*. The roles in question do require the presence of other comparable but unlike roles, since they would obviously not have been specifically named unless such a differentiation existed and was considered important. Thus one would not speak of 'Moslems' unless there are also non-Moslems to be considered, of 'Nupe', unless they coexist with other tribes, of 'old men' unless the viewpoint of age is also applicable to others, and so forth.[1] But no

---

[1] The absence in many primitive societies of collective names for their tribal or religious community seems a case in point. Where the 'We-group' is considered unique and its differentiation from others taken for granted, there is clearly no need to create a special 'role' indicating the class of people making up that collectivity.

role in this category implicates other roles beyond this minimum requirement of coexistence, as true counterparts necessary for its own enactment.

Conversely, fully relational roles also have their autonomous aspect. In this sense a 'father' can be independently defined, as a man to whom a child has been born, and a 'wife' as a woman who has a husband; a 'host' is a person who offers, or is capable of offering, hospitality to others; a 'patron', a person of such wealth or standing that he can have 'clients' or 'protegés'. We note that it is the possession of a counterpart role which is thus made the *differentia* for the independent definition of the relational role. In other words, we subject the relational role (E, for ego) to two viewpoints. From one, we see it as implicating a counterpart role (A, for alter) without which it cannot be enacted—

(15) $$E \supset A.$$

From the other, we make this implication the governing attribute of the role, possibly an achievement attribute, thus—

(16) $$E = \Sigma\, a \ldots p \ldots n, \text{ if } p \equiv E \supset A.$$

This means, as in the case of all governing attributes, that 'further characteristics' may go with it—some particular rights and obligations entailed in fatherhood, married status, and in being a host or patron.

This double aspect of relational roles, which I will call the *dichotomization* of roles, is, I suggest, of great importance. For it is not only we, the students of social systems, who can handle and look at roles in these two ways; the same is true of the societies possessing the roles in question. The importance of the dichotomization of roles then lies in this. The correlative aspect of any role (of whatever degree) relates it to a limited range of persons —the persons in the counterpart roles—towards whom the actor exercises the rights and obligations intrinsic to the role; while its autonomous aspects render it capable of being related beyond that range, beyond the 'enclaves' I spoke of before, to a wider (or widest) 'public'. No social system leaves the latter possibility unutilized. 'Fathers' (as men having children) or 'wives' (as woman having husbands) will assume duties and entitlements valid in the society at large, over and above those they have towards their children or husbands. 'Doctors' and 'priests' will be assigned parts which they will play *vis-à-vis* a public other (and wider) than their patients or congregation. Persons who are 'partners' or 'friends' to other persons may occupy a well defined, perhaps legalized status in wider contexts or groups; even of 'lovers' this might be true since, proverbially, they are loved 'by the whole world'. We may speak of these relationships of wider span as extrinsic or external, as against the relationships intrinsic to any given pair of correlative roles. The superimposition of the external relationship clearly helps to strengthen the coherence of role systems, and hence the integration of societies, even though the additional, external relationships may only be of the actor-public kind.

Needless to say, the external relationships do not cancel the intrinsic ones; on the contrary, they presuppose them. It is in consequence of their involvement in a reciprocal relationship that the persons playing the correlative roles are also involved in or provided with the additional relationships. Thus we might also speak, instead of the dichotomization of roles, of the *triadization* of relationships. For what happens here is that the dyadic relationship of persons in correlative roles comes to involve the interests and reactions of 'third parties'. It may do so, quite simply, because the dyadic relationship is concerned with providing goods or services needed by a 'third party', with managing a state of affairs affecting the interests of the latter or, more simply still, because it involves the co-operation of two persons *vis-à-vis* a third (or a plurality of 'third parties'). There are more indirect and subtle instances of triadization, when the enactment of the dyadic relationship falls in a moral sense within the purview of others—of potential critics, witnesses, a public of some kind.

In all these cases it is rarely the bare existence of the reciprocal relationship which thus evokes the interests and reactions of third parties, but its manner of enactment. In this sense the reciprocal relationship, as it obtains or should obtain by the norms of the society—between fathers and children, wives and husbands, doctors and patients, priests and believers, managers and employees, or between fellow workers—becomes the *concern* of actors in other roles. It determines their behaviour towards, and hence their relationships with, the persons in the reciprocal relationships, even if the 'other actors' are simply the rest of society. Conversely, the contingent reactions of the 'third party' also become the concern of the persons in the reciprocal relationship, guiding or influencing their mutual behaviour. In brief, one kind of relationship determines or implicates others. And this situation, as will be remembered, corresponds exactly to what I have called, early on, the *interlocking* of relationships and their expansion (their orderly expansion) ultimately into a *network*.

Writing once more E (ego) and A (alter) for the relational roles, and T for any actor or actors completing the 'triad', we can apply this brief calculus—

(17a)   if $E \supset A$ (and *vice versa*), so that
                  $E(a \ldots n): A$, and
                  $\therefore ErA$,

then, in virtue of the dichotomization of roles, there is a role T so that

(17b) $[E(a \ldots n)]: T$
                  $\therefore ErA \rightleftarrows Tr(E, A)$.

Formula (17b), then, symbolizes that crucial juncture in the coherence and orderliness of social structures, the interlocking of relationships. Differently expressed, it symbolizes the *transitiveness* of relationships. And I would argue, more generally, that when we try to trace the orderly interconnectedness of any plurality of relationships, such as might fill and 'hold together' a group or society, we shall find that it corresponds to the situation described by this set of formulae. It should perhaps be emphasized that though such a network might 'fill' a group or perhaps the whole society it does not, by itself, constitute it. For a group must have boundaries, a 'bounded area', while the mere interlocking of relationships produces an open-ended network, of the dispersed kind Barnes has in mind (see above, p. 17). We shall return to this point a little later.

Meanwhile it will be seen that, if the interlocking relationships really stretch across a group or society, the E, A and T in our formulae must be in the plural. Also, they must be understood to be widely interchangeable in that any E or A may become the T of other E's and A's. There are exceptions; there exist as it were professional and permanent T's—the holders of supervisory, controlling and authority roles, people acting officially for the public or the rest of society, and concerned in that capacity with the way in which other roles or relationships are executed.

A variety of crucial social phenomena hinges on the dichotomization of roles and on the consequent transitiveness of relationships. The facts just mentioned exemplify the link with the sanctioning machinery of social control. The 'politization' of roles, whereby the enactment of particular roles becomes the concern of the political authorities, is only a special case, involving the politically organized society as the 'third party' (see p. 82). As regards the effects upon social integration, dichotomization functions very similarly to the summation of roles. In a sense the two are alternative methods for achieving the same end: both extend the relationships in which actors would otherwise be involved—dichotomization, by adding a public to the so-to-speak more private aspects of role performance, and summation, by investing the same actor both with private and public roles. Now we have a special concept to denote this public aspect of roles; for when we say of persons that they have, gain or lose *prestige*, we indicate typical reactions of the public to the occupancy of given roles and to the way they are being played, estimably or not. The esteem, honour and deference (or the opposite) accorded to the role-playing actor are, from his point of view, the passive attributes of prestige; the corresponding active attributes lie in his command over the actions of others, who will follow his advice, pay attention to his wishes, and so on. In so far as prestige can increase or decrease in accordance with the performance of roles, it lends them some of that 'unfolding' character we discussed in an earlier context. Whether the prestige expands or declines, and whether it attaches to roles as such or to their variable performance, it means a measure of public 'concern', which in turn means a measure of dichotomization. In brief, when we speak of prestige we speak of the interlocking of relationships.

5

The most important consequence of dichotomization has to do with the interrelation of sub-groups. But before explaining this, I must digress a little.

The various relationships which we have so far considered all referred to situations where actors in different or complementary roles face one another. Obviously, this is not the only possibility. Individuals in unique roles or in roles having only few actors are, in the nature of things, surrounded by persons in unlike other roles. But there are a great many roles having large numbers of actors, so that these are all the time meeting persons in like roles. As in the case of logically related roles, the question arises how far the actors in like roles are also likely or perhaps bound to enter into determinate relationships with one another. This is again a purely empirical point, and unproblematic. But there is this to be considered. The presence of determinate relationships between actors in unlike roles (e.g. 'husbands' and 'wives', or 'musicians' and 'priests') indicates no more than that any member of one class of people is linked, by rules of mutual behaviour, with any member of another class of people. The presence, however, of determinate relationships between actors in like roles (all 'husbands', 'wives', 'musicians', 'priests') indicates something new, namely a bounded area of relationships, the extent of the likeness being also the extent (and forming the boundary) of the relationships. In other words, such relationships indicate that here a class of people is also an organized group, as we understand the term.

Needless to say, a class of people in the society, sharing some attribute or series of attributes, is not for that reason also a 'group' viz. sub-group: it becomes one when 'class' equals 'role' (or quasi-role) and, more important, when being of a like kind goes with being 'held together' by relationships. The distinction is sometimes obscured when the shared attributes are such that they already suggest shared relationships, either owing to linguistic usage or owing to common experience. Thus we tend to describe a collection of people descended in the same line, unhappily suggestively, as 'relations by descent', as we also speak of consanguinary or agnatic 'relationships'; and true it is that the shared attribute of lineal descent commonly entails genuine relationships in the sense of mutual behaviour. But strictly speaking, a collection of agnates or any other 'relations' is only a class of people and not *ipso facto* a sub-group.[1]

But this is by the way. As regards classes of people which do in fact coincide with sub-groups proper, it is clear that no society completely disregards this possibility of constructing unity out of uniformity or likeness. And if the coincidence is automatic and complete, so that playing a given role is coterminous with belonging to the respective sub-group, we may expect the ordinary role name tacitly to imply the group membership. This is a familiar case. In our own society, for example a 'soldier' is always a member of an army (while 'warrior' in a primitive society may indicate only a class of people and an independent role). Again, from our knowledge of a particular society we shall understand that being a 'youth' always means being a member of an age-grade association, being a 'craftsman', a member of a guild or caste, or being a 'priest', belonging to a religious order.

But sub-groups are not necessarily formed in this way. Often, they are so constructed that they draw their personnel from diverse classes of people and recruit their members indirectly, *via* some previous role or series of roles. Usually (and logically) special names will then indicate the group membership thus superimposed upon an originally differentiated human material—names such as trade unionist, freemason, Fellow of the Royal Society, or of any other association, club and the like.

Let me add in parenthesis that membership of the society at large, that is, citizenship, is not of this kind, even though it suggests a similar superimposition of unity upon diversity. Unless we think of newly emerged political units, conquest states, and the like, the society does not really 'draw' its personnel from all the diverse classes of people found in it; rather it *is* all these classes of people, its norms allowing for them and indeed providing them, as modes of existence available for 'citizens'.

This account of the formation of groups and sub-groups

---

[1] The use of 'lineage' in modern anthropological literature exemplifies a confusion of this kind; for it often leaves it uncertain whether one means a mere class of people, on the grounds of common descent, or an organized ('corporate') sub-group of the society.

could undoubtedly be expanded. It should also be observed that the formation of any sub-group in turn entails the formation of a new class of people, now sharing the sub-group membership as their common attribute; so that the process whereby unity is created out of (pre-existing) likeness is in a sense reversible. But all this is of minor importance.

What is important is that belonging to a sub-group, being involved in its regular activities and rules of behaviour, has all the characteristics of role performance. Which means that the names describing persons in terms of the sub-groups they belong to are true role names. And this means, further, that these membership roles, whether explicitly named or not, correspond to *relational* roles, since the very nature of groups depends on the relationships between the people composing them. It makes no sense to speak of the 'member' of a group unless there are others also, or of his particular rights and obligations in the sub-group unless they implicate corresponding rights and obligations on the part of fellow members. In other words, each membership role posits, in the manner of relational roles, actors in counterpart roles, its own efficacy and realism depending on their presence.

Basically, this 'positing' of other roles refers to like roles—to other soldiers, trade unionists, freemasons, and so forth. For even if the sub-group has been constructed out of originally unlike roles, the original differentiation belongs to the recruitment phase, to the 'prehistory' of the membership role, and is more or less efficiently superseded by the new status. Admittedly there may be a further differentiation of functions in the sub-group, whichever way it is recruited, as when kin groups have a head, not only ordinary members, and a trade union a lodge of freemasons, or the Royal Society their officers and functionaries. But this differentiation can be regarded as additional to the common sub-group membership and as presupposing it. At the same time this differentiation produces once more roles and definable relationships between them. These are now located primarily in a subdivision of the society and only secondarily in the society at large. Differently put, sub-groups have an internal order, a 'structure' of their own.

The question arises, how far this order has a 'secondary'

validity, in the society at large. If we think of an extreme case, a highly esoteric or perhaps secret association, its internal roles and relationships will have no such validity, being possibly even unknown outside the association. All that is likely to be known about its personnel and taken into account by the general public would be the bare fact of membership. The other extreme is exemplified by such membership roles as President of the Royal Society or Trade Union Secretary. These roles clearly have that 'secondary' validity, being public roles as well as roles indicating the internal differentiation valid in the sub-group.

6

This brings me to the crucial point in this somewhat devious argument, the transition from the strictly relational aspect of membership roles, from their internal or 'inward' efficacy as it were, to their external and 'outward' validity. In so far as there is such a transition, it rests, once more, on the dichotomization of the respective roles. Through it, the actors are placed in relationships with other actors outside their sub-group, ultimately with the society at large. Often the 'other actors' will again be members of sub-groups; and these, like the membership roles, may be like or unlike, repetitive or differentiated. In the first case, members of one clan, trade union or lodge of freemasons will act towards members of other clans, trade unions or lodges; in the second, trade unionists will act *vis-à-vis* employers, and freemasons *vis-à-vis* religious or political bodies, and so on.

In a sense this is merely restating the familiar juxtaposition of in-group and out-group relationships. But we are restating it with a special emphasis, not on the mere coexistence of these two alignments, but on their interlocking or, more precisely, their complementary nature. For the character of the outward (or 'out-group') actions and relationships is still determined by group membership and membership roles; it is in virtue of the latter, in consequence of the rights and obligations assumed in the 'in-group', that the actors also exhibit their characteristic behaviour towards people outside or are met with characteristic behaviour by them. The two are simply sides of the same coin. If the members of a clan are expected to collaborate, compete or intermarry with members of other clans; if trade unionists are expected to bargain with employers; and if a freemason is expected to attack the Church, this is so precisely because these men are clansfellows, trade unionists, freemasons.

The 'because' in this sentence covers a variety of possibilities of which these three are probably the main ones. (i) Certain sub-groups will be specifically designed so as to enable the people so joined together (in trade unions, co-operatives, and other associations based on common interests) to manage their dealings with others, and to manage them more efficiently than they could if they acted independently. Here, then, the sub-group has *ab initio* an outward focus, the inward relationships and interactions (its 'syncretic' activities) representing the means whereby to achieve the aimed-at, external ones. (ii) Other sub-groups have an inward focus, upon the 'togetherness' they afford in virtue of the syncretic rights and obligations; they assume particular outward relationships owing to distributive factors, that is, owing to some restriction of entitlements and facilities available within the sub-group. Think of clans which, by their rule of exogamy, must seek their marriage partners outside, or of group segments which depend on one another's services or skills owing to the obtaining division of labour. Here the outward relationships are the means, the end being the continued existence of the 'togetherness' under the prevailing ('distributive') conditions. On the widest scale, involving each segment and thus the whole subdivided society, this situation corresponds to a 'symbiotic' interdependence or interrelation. (iii) Finally, the outward efficacy might simply be the obverse of the internal togetherness. The former might then take the form of characteristic 'diacritical' behaviour *vis-à-vis* outsiders, meant to signal the identity and unity of the sub-group. Or again, the outward efficacy will follow from some ideology fostered within the sub-group, meant to sustain its solidarity and collective loyalties and inevitably involving notions or value judgments about 'strangers' and 'outsiders'.[1]

Needless to say, there will be some overlap between these

---

[1] The terms *syncretic*, *symbiotic*, and *diacritical* were introduced in my contribution to *African Systems of Kinship and Marriage*, p. 337. See also my *Foundations*, pp. 157, 179.

possibilities. Also, the outward efficacy they involve will vary widely in specificity or generality. One extreme would be marked by outward relationships which are the precise counterparts of inward ones ('marriage outside, no marriage inside', 'conflict without, solidarity within'); the other, by outward relationships of a highly generalized order, involving only broad rules of conduct *vis-à-vis* 'outsiders' (aloofness, 'keeping one's station', diffuse sympathy or hostility). There is no need to elaborate this outline further. Nor need we concern ourselves with the kind of outward efficacy which is purely negative, tending towards the mutual isolation of sub-groups through enjoining on their members strict hostility towards or segregation from others. The main object of this discussion was to show, very generally, that the relational character of group roles, linking the actors with one another (or 'inwards'), is balanced by a further relational factor, whereby the group members are linked 'outward', with other sub-groups or the society at large—with 'third parties' of some order or description.

A similar point is made by Parsons, Bales and Shils when they speak of 'internal' roles or role aspects, which represent 'that aspect of the total role in which ego is acting *vis-à-vis* other members of the organization'; by contrast, the 'representational' aspects of the group role cause ego to act 'on behalf of the organization *vis-à-vis* non-members'.[1] Perhaps the phrase 'on behalf of' introduces a wrong perspective, suggesting that all 'external' actions or relationships are in some measure delegated ones. This obviously need not be the case. I would regard such actions as a special case of that broader 'outward efficacy' which pertains to all group roles. And this, in turn, I regard as a special case of the still wider principle, the dichotomization of all roles having a relational significance. Applied to membership roles, dichotomization enables sub-groups to be 'bounded areas of relationships', with all the solidarity and self-containedness implied in that condition, while yet maintaining vital outside links. Once more, the principle of dichotomization subserves the overall social integration; it conforms to the twofold nature of sub-groups, which are discrete units without being isolates or rigid 'enclaves'; differently expressed, it explains the

[1] See *Working Papers*, p. 261.

fundamental fact about sub-groups, that they exhibit both an internal and external 'system' (Homans) or 'order' (Nadel).

This external system or order clearly helps to build up the overall orderliness of societies. It does so in the manner in which we found relationships to be interrelated, through the dichotomous aspect of roles and the consequent interlocking of relationships, ultimately in a network. What is novel about this overall orderliness is that its units are formal subdivisions of the society, i.e. 'bounded areas' within it; it is not made up merely of an infinite array of relationships, interconnected and 'filling up' the society. Yet we must not think of two discrete levels of this interlocking or visualize two complementary scales of network, one showing relationships held together in sub-groups, the other, sub-groups held together in the society at large. Neat and tempting though this picture may be, it is inaccurate; for relationships may interlock without being first confined in sub-groups, with the society at large as their locus, as was amply documented by our examples. The two networks, in other words, can exist side by side and interpenetrate. They differ in one respect: one connects bounded units and is itself bounded, while the other is 'open-ended'. But the important thing is that they both *are* networks, constructed on the same principle.

To say it again, the interrelation of sub-groups is coterminous with the relationship of persons in their (dichotomous) membership roles. Let me emphasize that in reducing the interrelation of sub-groups to the relationships of actors in their roles I am not merely trying to simplify the picture and to reduce a variety of factors to a common formula. Disregarding the linkage by recruitment and the rare occasions of genuinely collective actions, there is no other way to give meaning to the conception of interrelations between groups. In so far as they are relations resting on interaction, they rest on the interactions of individual members—interactions which take their particular form because the actors are members of their respective groups and act in that corporate capacity, as *representatives* of their group and in accordance with group rules. It is only a loose way of speaking to say that there is collaboration or hostility between whole clans, between trade unions and employers, or between freemasons and the Church. What we really mean is that such are the norms valid in each group and dictating the way its members (in that role) should behave *vis-à-vis* the members of the other group (in their roles); the 'external' efficacy of the norms is then visible whenever the individuals meet or find occasion to interact, by chance or by the very design of the norm.

All this has a final consequence. If it is correct to reduce the interrelation of sub-groups to the interrelation of actors in their roles, then the cleavages and barriers standing in the way of the latter must hold for the former also. It is hardly necessary to prove this. Obviously, sub-groups, like roles, can be logically disparate (e.g. kin groups and age grades); they can be factually dissociated (any two sub-groups which have no dealings with one another); or they may retain their character of 'enclaves' (as in the case of esoteric or secret associations). Thus, though we now know what kinds of overall interconnections to expect we can predict nothing about the scale or comprehensiveness of the resulting 'network', save certain negative facts, namely that it is bound to have gaps and breaks at every level. It seems helpful to restate these facts briefly, from a somewhat different angle.

V

DEGREES OF ABSTRACTION

THE definition of social structure which we made our starting point stipulated the ordered arrangement, system or network of the social relationships obtaining between individuals 'in their capacity of playing roles relative to one another'. We therefore regarded the role system of any society, with its given coherence, as the matrix of the social structure. But we found this matrix broken up by logical cleavages and by the factual dissociation of roles. More simply stated, a great many actors never can 'play their roles relative to one another', simply because the roles have no common locus, logically or empirically. The absence of a common logical locus precludes the assumption of a unitary, coherent system; indeed, there seem to be as many separate systems as there are logical role frames. Between them, there is only the linkage provided by recruitment rules, defining the flow or 'circulation' of persons between disparate sets of roles and the chances of their belonging to several at once. Where the logical cleavages are absent, the factual dissociation of roles still makes it impossible to relate certain roles with one another since the actors in these roles never meet in that capacity in social intercourse. Rather, one of the actors in his role would face a more or less broad public, of indeterminate role composition, so that the 'ordered arrangement' of relationships contains so-to-speak zones of indeterminacy. Finally, the relational or correlative character of roles will tend to isolate the respective relationships from one another, in the manner of enclaves. The result, then, is that our 'ordered arrangement', far from being a total one, must remain fragmentary. In a word, it seems impossible to speak of a social structure in the singular.

Let me show this graphically. If there were such a thing as a fully coherent role system and a unitary social structure, a role system containing roles belonging to two different logical frames (a, b, c, d and α, β, γ, δ) could be represented in a matrix every cell of which would be filled, thus:

Fig. 1

	a	b	c	d	α	β	γ	δ
a		+	+	+	+	+	+	+
b	+		+	+	+	+	+	+
c	+	+		+	+	+	+	+
d	+	+	+		+	+	+	+
α	+	+	+	+		+	+	+
β	+	+	+	+	+		+	+
γ	+	+	+	+	+	+		+
δ	+	+	+	+	+	+	+	

The logical cleavages on the other hand, since they preclude relationships between logically disparate roles, would introduce blank spaces, thus:

Fig. 2

	a	b	c	d	α	β	γ	δ
a		+	+	+				
b	+		+	+				
c	+	+		+				
d	+	+	+					
α						+	+	+
β					+		+	+
γ					+	+		+
δ					+	+	+	

The reduction of role-to-role relationships to relationships of the actor-public kind, though it would fill the matrix, would fill it in an indeterminate fashion, the former links being submerged in the collective orientations upon 'customers', 'audience', 'congregation', or simply 'the rest of society'. This may be indicated in the following fashion:

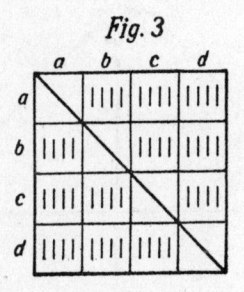

Fig. 3

And the enclaves produced by correlative roles would give this picture (a-a, b-c, d-d being three such pairs of roles, like and unlike, e.g. friend-friend, host-guest, freemason-freemason):

Fig. 4

This lack of coherence and unity in any presumed social structure might not apply to the same degree if we changed our whole approach and considered the attachment of relationships to concrete persons, to the Toms, Dicks and Harrys of any society, rather than to the roles they choose or are made to play. For in view of the possible summation of roles, concrete individuals, unrelated to one another in the sense of certain of their roles, might yet be related in the sense of others. We could in fact think of situations where a whole set of people, considered as total persons, exhibits a fully coherent, single network of relationships while the analysis of their roles would yield only

100 THE THEORY OF SOCIAL STRUCTURE

one that is discontinuous or fragmentary. The model below illustrates such a situation for four persons, A, B, C and D:

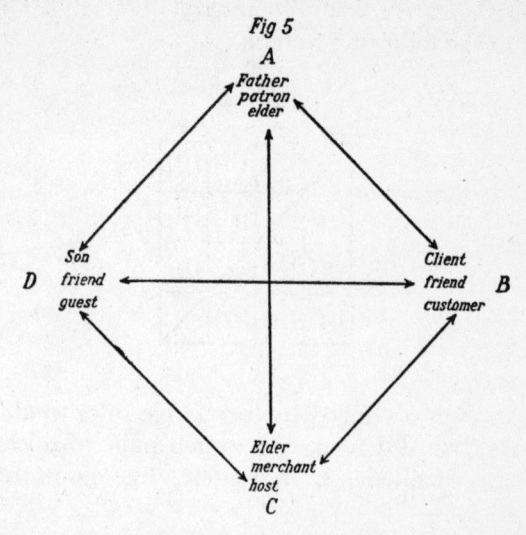

Fig 5

```
            A
        Father
        patron
        elder

  Son                    Client
D friend                 friend  B
  guest                  customer

           Elder
           merchant
           host
             C
```

But this cannot mean that we should give up talking about roles and actor relationships and refer instead to concrete people and the ties between them, because by this method we shall find it easier to construct a coherent 'structure'. Nor am I exaggerating the difficulties of this task—difficulties readily overcome if we are prepared to change our methods. For the approach through person-to-person relationships can only imply one of two things. Either it leads to provisional findings, leaving it unexplained on what principle (by what 'brief') the individuals in question actually assume their various relationships: which means that the enquiry into the role-to-role connections is only postponed. Or the approach means, if we also disregard the principles or 'brief' underlying the relationship, that we are treating them as purely 'personal' and accidental occurrences, concerning particular people in particular circumstances: which is not what we have agreed to understand by 'social structure'.

In a sense, however, I have been exaggerating the lack of coherence in any given social structure; for to some extent it will be corrected or rendered less relevant by a number of

DEGREES OF ABSTRACTION

factors. Thus in simple, homogeneous societies certain of the 'blanks' in the structure will not matter; since, in such societies, numerous roles, including disparate ones, invariably coincide (we remember our paradigm, the family head-cum-manager-cum-priest), the need to trace relationships between the persons playing these roles simply does not arise. Again, a high degree of 'personalization' will partly eliminate or reduce some of the 'zones of indeterminacy'. And dichotomization will bridge the mutually isolated enclaves. But for the society as a whole, for the total collection of existing roles and relationships, these gaps and breaks cannot be entirely spirited away. More important, even where they do not apply, perhaps in selected, restricted sectors of social life, other difficulties will arise. We may indeed know that all the roles we are concerned with (for example, in such a selected sector) are linked in relationships and that all the relationships combine to form a single network. If so, it would seem that all we have to do is to describe or somehow indicate the character—the *orderly* character—of the combination. But to be able to do this we must deal with data which are in fact comparable and 'combinable'. And it is here that we meet with new obstacles.

Let us consider a small area of roles and relationships (another 'miniature system') represented by the nuclear family, that is, by the set of roles exemplified by a man ('father' and 'husband'), his wife ('wife' and 'mother'), and say two sons ('sons' and 'brothers'). There are, of course, no cleavages or lacunae in this situation; all roles are interrelated, both logically and through actual behaviour. We have in fact that most coherent network, corresponding to a full matrix:

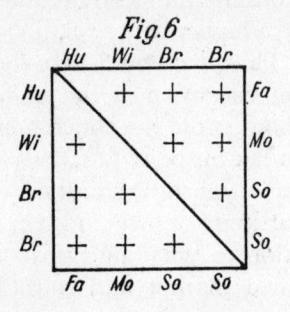

Fig.6

	Hu	Wi	Br	Br	
Hu	\	+	+	+	Fa
Wi	+	\	+	+	Mo
Br	+	+	\	+	So
Br	+	+	+	\	So
	Fa	Mo	So	So	

Here if anywhere our data should prove entirely comparable and combinable. Yet while we continue to think of roles and relationships in the way we have done so far, this is simply not the case.

Roles, we remember, were for us series of behavioural attributes, each with its peculiar content of aims, tasks, expectations, entitlements, obligations; relationships in turn referred to the constancies of behaviour, still conceived with this kind of content, between people described in role terms. In other words, all our formulae had to contain the letters a, b, c ... n, indicative of the particular contents and qualities. Now from this point of view the relationship between a father and a son implies 'paternal' care and authority and 'filial' respect and love, and would lose its very identity without this implication; the relationship between husband and wife implies, among other things, sexual intimacy; the relationship between brothers, sibling rivalry or solidarity. Obviously, this list can be extended further, to include many other qualities. The point is that it always does include qualities, and hence *differentiae* of an irreducible nature. How then can we combine them in some overall design? Or how can we extract, even from this miniature system, any embracing order while still paying attention to these qualitative characteristics? As it stands, each relationship contains unique features which render it incomparable with the others, offering nothing in the way of a common criterion or dimension. All we can do, apparently, is to enumerate and describe the diverse relationships and place them side by side, as so many disparate entities.

We can in fact do a little more; for we can indicate also the interlocking of relationships and thus the extension of the dyadic to triadic and perhaps higher-order relationships, ultimately to the whole network. Thus we should note the 'concern' of each parent in the proper execution of the sibling relationship, as seen by them. We should note the concern of the mother in the relationship between her husband and the sons, which might be such as to express an authoritarian and disciplinarian attitude, as against her own attitude of love and care. The father would similarly pay attention to what he considers the appropriate relationship between a mother and sons. In either case the husband-wife relationship would be adjusted to and affected by the relationship of each towards the children. The sibling relationship in turn would be determined by the particular attitude of the parents towards each sibling, say, partiality towards a younger son; and each son-parent relationship would be determined by the enactment of the relationship between the parents, for example, by any disturbance of the latter by quarrels, jealousy, infidelity, etc.

But this picture is still too heavily invested with qualitative features to yield any clear order or overall design. Though the picture does indicate a complete and coherent network, with all its strands interlocking, the very ways and points of interlocking retain a great deal that is pure 'quality'. The mother's concern over her husband's harshness or mildness towards the sons; the parents' concern over the brotherly feelings of the sons; and the sons' concern over the marital relations of their parents—all these are still incomparable and, from the point of view of any overall order, intractable. Again, all that we seem able to do is to enumerate and describe separately each triadic or higher-order relationship.

If we were to extend the system of kinship roles, this would not necessarily mean a proportionate increase in the incomparability of the relationships involved, simply because some of the added relationships would prove to be identical or similar to those contained in the miniature system. For example, the father's brother's relationships with his brother's sons might merely duplicate (or approximately duplicate) the father-son relationship. Yet where this extension beyond the miniature system implies the inclusion of differentiated roles and relationships, the 'intractability' we discussed a moment ago will in fact be increased. And much the same intractability would characterize any other coherent role system. Think of the diversified relationships and their ways of interlocking involved in any productive enterprise of some complexity (which would include managers, foremen, consultants, and workers in different or like tasks), or in any political-administrative set-up, with its diverse offices, responsibilities and channels of communication. Even in a relatively simple organization like a school there will be the diverse and incomparable relationships between teachers, between teachers and pupils, between the pupils, and between the parents and the teachers.

2

I have said enough about what seem to me the difficulties of building up an overall order or structure from roles and relationships defined with full regard to their qualitative content or character. Now it might once more be objected that I am exaggerating the difficulties, that is, that I am exaggerating the logical requirements of such a total 'order'. This order, it might be argued, need not be a simple one and so-to-speak unidimensional. The kind of network we outlined before (and dismissed as intractable) might be all we need, being in no way vitiated by the qualitative diversity of the respective relationships and their ways of interlocking. The kinship structure, the structure of a productive enterprise, an administration or school, would simply be the sum total of the varying relationships (of whatever order), and we should find the total 'design' —a perfectly satisfactory one—in their particular combination and juxtaposition.

My answer would be that such a treatment would destroy the crucial character of structure as here understood, namely, its transposibility. A design of this kind could never be freely transposed to a different kind of material, say, from kinship data to the data describing some political or religious organization. Yet it is precisely this transposibility which makes structural studies useful (apart from the fact that the meaning of 'structure' requires it). Nor do the defenders of structural studies fail to stress this kind of usefulness: they mean nothing else when they underline the great value of the concept of structure for comparative analysis. We shall return to this argument later. Let me here give a simple example to illustrate my point.

In his book *The Human Group* Homans draws an interesting comparison between the Tikopian and Trobriand family, thereby illustrating a principle of kinship organization which has been recognized, though not as explicitly or in quite the same terms, by many anthropologists. In Tikopia the father-son relationship is characterized by some degree of remoteness, formality, and constraint, resting as it does on respect-obedience rather than affection-friendliness, while the latter attitude is characteristic of the relationship between a youth and his mother's brother. In the Trobriands this position is by and large reversed. In each case, as Homans points out, we have the same juxtaposition of two relationships, one disciplinarian, the other friendly, one indicating superiority-subordination, the other equality, which link men in junior and senior generations in two opposed but balanced ways. And since this juxtaposition occurs in different kinship systems, different, that is, at least as regards the precise allocation of the relationships in question, Homans concludes that, in fact, the 'system' is the same 'if we forget about biological kinship . . . and look at the working group instead'.[1] We should say, perhaps more correctly, that what is identical in the two cases is the kinship 'structure' (or part of it), and what we 'forget about', the different human and role material in which it is embodied. We note, incidentally, that in order to express the very juxtaposition we also had to disregard (or forget about) the full content of each dyadic relationship. We were obviously not considering the complete character of the father-son relationship as compared with that between mother's brother and sister's son; rather, we extracted from the two relationships only those general attributes which belong to a common dimension (authority-friendliness or superiority-equality) and for that reason prove comparable or combinable.

Now similar 'structures', including other roles besides (e.g. the role of a 'friendly' grandfather), are well known from many other kinship systems. Indeed, we might follow up a suggestion of Homans's and ask if the particular balance typical of kin groups does not represent an even more basic principle, likely to govern also the structure of any other groupings similarly involving relationships between people in superior and subordinate positions.[2] There too, we might hypothesize, we should find an authoritarian relationship being juxtaposed with and balanced by an amicable, egalitarian one. Why this should be so is a question which, in this context, we may disregard. But if we were to set out to find evidence for such a hypothesis, we

[1] Op. cit. 1951, pp. 248-51, 258.
[2] Op. cit., pp. 260-1.

should have to 'forget' much more than merely the rules for the allocation of the two complementary relationships. If we were to consider in this light, say, political or business organizations, our task would be stultified if we retained the relationships of our paradigm with their full qualitative character. The particular connotation of 'disciplinarian' in the father-son relationship, and the particular 'friendliness' of a mother's brother or grandfather playing or joking with his nephew or grandson, are obviously not 'transposable'. So that the comparisons for the purpose of testing our hypothesis would have to stop before they started.

We must, then, view and describe the relationships to be compared quite differently. In our example it is perhaps enough to employ the attributes 'disciplinarian' and 'friendly' in a highly general sense, giving no thought to the more specific features; or we might have to go further in emptying the relationships of quality and content, and speak only of 'subordination' and 'equality'. However this may be, the example proves, I think, that in presenting a social structure without reducing the qualitative character of the component relationships we should fail in two respects: not only would it be impossible to combine them satisfactorily in a single order, but it would also be futile to try and transpose that order (such as it would be in the circumstances).

3

To reduce qualitative features and to disregard the characteristics of particular cases is to apply some method of *abstraction*. This, we might note, is our third level of abstraction. We began by disregarding the varying concrete instances of behaviour between people in order to define the constant linkages, the relationships between them. Again, we abstracted these from the concrete living beings performing them, thus proceeding from individuals and populations to actors in roles and relationships. We must now drive abstraction a stage further, beyond the qualitative character of the roles and actor relationships. In other words, we must get rid of the a, b, c . . . n in our formulae. Which means employing criteria of a rigorously formal and relational kind.

Just how rigorous should our third-level abstraction be? As I shall argue later, the answer to this question can only be a fairly arbitrary one, dictated by considerations of expediency. But certain of these can perhaps be stated in general terms. To begin with, the criterion to be employed must not be such that it applies to relationships as to self-contained, autonomous units, indicating only their similarity and dissimilarity. Such a criterion would yield only a distributive pattern, not yet a network. Assume, for example, that we used the dimension 'discipline-friendliness': we should then be able to say of a given nuclear family only that it contains, in a total of six possible relationships, four which are 'friendly' (father-mother, mother-elder son, mother-younger son, brother-brother), and two which are 'disciplinarian' (father-elder son, father-younger son). Or take a different criterion—parental care and control: it only enables us to indicate that four relationships are of this kind (father towards each son, mother towards each son), while the remaining two are incomparable with these and with each other (husband-wife, brother-brother). To be more profitable, then, our criterion must refer not to the 'inward' aspect of relationships (which makes them self-contained units, combinable only in a distributive pattern), but to their 'outward' aspect, whereby they become interconnected. In other words, our criterion must be capable of indicating the 'concern' that underlies the triadization of relationships, and hence their transitiveness.

It will readily be seen that this concern is itself a product of abstraction. But to rely on it alone would once more be unprofitable, now because the abstraction would go too far. The picture of the social structure presented on this basis would show little more than the mere presence of interrelations between relationships. It would confirm that these 'second-order relations' combine in a network, of such and such coherence. And there probably are occasions when this kind of evidence is relevant and sufficient. This would be the case, for example, when we wish to indicate the varying degree of closure and completeness of two networks, comparing, say, a complete and relatively closed network (as in the nuclear family) and one that is open-ended and interrupted (e.g. the kindred or a man's set of friends, not all of whom may know each other). But this mere presentation of the ways and degrees of interlocking is too uninformative for our purpose, even in a strictly structural analysis. We surely need a little more content and substance. If the first criterion we discussed was unprofitable because it did not indicate the transitiveness of relationships, the second fails because it indicates nothing else. We conclude that the desirable level of abstraction lies somewhere in between, being non-qualitative, relational or 'formal', but not excessively so.

Now this search, apart from having so indefinite a goal, also involves us in linguistic difficulties. For we have no special words to distinguish relationships still carrying a definite qualitative content ('paternal care', 'filial respect', 'discipline', 'friendliness') from others which leave it behind or, as I put it elsewhere, 'bracket it away'. Even less have we words to define different levels or degrees of this 'bracketing away'. Thus we must continue to speak, very broadly, of relationships, noting only their greater or lesser abstractness or 'formal' character. At the same time we have an appropriate choice of terms for roles which are similarly emptied of qualitative content; for here we may say that in this process roles (or 'statuses') turn into mere *positions*. And what we usually do is to borrow this term in order to describe relationships of a high degree of abstractness. In this sense we can say of our third level of abstraction that it is one at which relationships mean relative position and little else. If, from the start, we envisaged social structure as a 'positional picture', we have now indicated, if only roughly, the level of abstraction to which it must correspond.

Now I suggested that we merely 'borrow' the term position to indicate relationships emptied of all qualitative features; I did not mean to imply that we subject the roles involved to the same process. Indeed, we could not do so without being caught in tautologies. We must still view social structure as being built out of relationships between persons in their roles. This seems to contradict Radcliffe-Brown's thesis that social structure has to do with 'positions', not with 'roles'—the latter belonging to a different frame of reference, that of 'organization'.[1] Yet if we thus emptied both roles and relationships of their qualitative content, we should be moving in a circle. It makes sense, for

[1] *Structure and Function in Primitive Society*, p. 11.

example, to say that a father stands 'above' his son, or a priest 'above' the layman: these are positional relationships expressed in terms of role-playing actors. If we now reduced the roles as well to mere positions, then all we could describe would be relationships of superordination or subordination between 'superiors' and 'inferiors'. At best, this double 'emptying-out' would lead to highly general—and purely distributive—statements, e.g. about societies being so divided, in strata or sections, that certain people (undefined) occupy particular positions *vis-à-vis* other persons (undefined). But let me add that this restriction upon our progress towards an abstract, purely positional picture is only temporary. Radcliffe-Brown's conception of structure is basically correct, though we need further tools to develop it. And these will be suggested a little later.

For the moment, our aim in moving to the third level of abstraction is to find criteria whereby we can demonstrate the positional picture presented by a collection of people enacting their various roles relative to one another. Obviously, we shall try to make this picture as comprehensive as possible and to get as near as we can to an overall arrangement or order. Here, however, we must remember our other difficulty, the zones of indeterminacy created by the factual dissociation of roles. Now I shall try to show that we can employ two closely related and consistent criteria which overcome both this difficulty and the incomparability of actually interconnected roles and relationships. In either case, and by similar methods, it will be possible to construct a relatively embracing role-to-role network or structure, if at some cost of descriptive fullness. Let me stress that the resulting structure is only relatively embracing, and still fragmentary; for it neither bridges the (unbridgeable) logical cleavages nor entirely removes the enclaves constituted by correlative roles. But before suggesting my own criteria I propose to discuss three other methods developed in modern sociology and social psychology, which similarly succeed in abstracting a purely relational or positional picture from concrete human relationships.

(I) *Sociometry*

4

The first method centres upon the most basic feature of group existence—the 'togetherness' of individuals as it becomes apparent in their spontaneous aggregation and segregation. The operative criteria are thus the 'moving towards' and the 'moving away' from one another of individuals face-to-face in collectivities. This method, developed by Moreno and his followers, aims ultimately at producing diagrammatic and geometricized representations (*sociograms*) of these moves and their results. Typical situations for which this is done are the choice of companions among inmates of some institution, the 'going-about-with-each-other' of schoolchildren, and their readiness to follow a leader in play groups and similar aggregates. The varying character of the relationships so emerging (friendship, companionship, other forms of 'sociation') is relatively unimportant. What counts in the relational pattern that emerges is the sheer positional definition of the places individuals occupy within it. Such places vary all the way down from the 'sociometric star', i.e. the individual chosen as a companion or leader by the majority, to the 'isolate', the individual left out from all the choices.

The strictly structural character of this method of analysis needs no emphasis. The students of sociometry would in fact describe their diagrams, maps, and measurements as demonstrating social structure. But used by itself, this method with its paramount criterion of 'sociation' is clearly inadequate for the analysis of real, full-scale societies. For one thing, it deals only with face-to-face relationships and with relationships restricted to single situations or strictly repetitive ones; and for another, it deals with situations where the qualitative variety of behaviour *ab initio* approximates to the purely 'relational' features aimed at in the analysis so that the problem of abstracting the latter from the former is an unusually easy one. For the individual behaviour in the contexts examined implies little more than wishing to be with so-and-so, subordinating oneself to so-and-so (or gaining ascendancy over him), and so on, that is, the kind of characteristics relevant for a social structure based solely on 'sociation'. In other words, the situation selected for observation is such that it contains the social structure to be analysed ready-made.

But though the method and the social structure which it produces are, from our point of view, inadequate since they oversimplify the normal conditions of analysis, they do point to factors relevant also in the kind of situations we must consider; for sociation of a given degree enters into every actor relationship and helps to define its character. A leadership involving mainly indirect and few face-to-face contacts clearly differs significantly from one resting mainly on the latter, even if in other respects the two are identical. The design of groups is similarly characterized by the amount of 'sociation' they offer or require. Even the 'service' relationships of poets or merchants require for their adequate description some reference to the physical 'togetherness' involved. Thus, whatever 'relational' criterion we shall select, it must be supplemented by such a reference or, in Lundberg's phrase, a 'sociation index'.[1]

(II) *Interaction Frequency*

This criterion was elaborated with considerable skill by Eliot Chapple and Homans.[2] With its help it is possible to isolate from any interpersonal relationship the sheer process of interaction, physical or verbal, in disregard of any other characteristics. The relative 'position' of the actors, in whatever roles they may face one another, can then be stated in terms of the proportion of their 'originating' or 'responding' actions, and the character of their relationship, in terms of interaction rates, synchronization, and of the 'equilibrium' or 'disequilibrium' characterizing the interaction process.

The attractiveness of this method lies not only in the thoroughness of the abstraction employed but also in the easy quantification, and hence comparability, of the results. Nor need the method be restricted to face-to-face situations, even though these usually furnish the majority of examples. Yet I would question whether interaction rates and the rest succeed in representing relationships in any significant way. As we agreed, abstraction from qualities and content there must be; my doubts are whether there are not more important things to abstract. Have we really seized upon the relevant difference (or

---

[1] G. A. Lundberg, *Social Research*, 1949, pp. 336, 338.
[2] See Eliot Chapple and C. S. Coon, *Principles of Anthropology*, 1942, pp. 36-41; G. C. Homans, *The Human Group*, 1951, pp. 35-7 et passim.

similarity) between the relationships father-son and husband-wife when we count and compare the respective interaction rates? And does it make much sense to define the positional picture of a group by assigning to each member an interaction-coefficient relative to every other member?

Let us admit that these things do make sense under very special conditions, such as hold in the highly specific and restricted studies usually undertaken by the students of 'interaction process'. But these conditions fail to apply in the broader anthropological field. The first is that the relationships studied should be such that overt behaviour exhausts their whole significance. Now this would be true of work groups, of groups met in discussion, and of similar situations. But compare in this manner the position, say, of a chief whose interactions with his subjects are severely circumscribed by taboos and rules of etiquette but whose tacit presence and office will influence and guide the conduct of the subjects, with that of a 'poor man' or 'outcast', who is isolated from general social life in a different sense; clearly, by mere interaction rates the two vastly different positions might well prove to be identical. Furthermore, the study of interaction, to be meaningful, presupposes activities whose aim content is held constant or taken for granted: again, the study of work groups, of debates, or of ceremonials offers examples. This condition limits the usefulness of the method entirely to single or to strictly repetitive situations, and to the roles and relationships operative in them. As soon as we go beyond them, as in our kind of study we must, the problem of comparability once more arises, and can be ignored only at the risk of producing a meaningless picture. In ritual contexts, for example, the interactions of a priest with his congregation will be high, and he will probably appear as the 'originator' of most of them; but in everyday life the position may well be reversed. The position of a craftsman *vis-à-vis* his customers on one side, and *vis-à-vis* his fellow villagers on the other, may show the same high-low interaction pattern. Do the two men therefore occupy an identical place in the social structure? And is the position of each to be defined in terms of the mean interaction, of its maximum, or of its minimum?

These are clearly nonsensical questions, nonsensical because the different interactions are not comparable, having a different quality, that is, a different weight or meaning in the lives of the individuals and of the whole society. In other words, we are back at the problem, how to abstract, in a profitable manner, form and relations from content and quality.

The disregard of content and meaning by the students of 'interaction process' is undoubtedly deliberate. But it is not easy to say just how far they are prepared to press it. In theory, at least, and in one respect, they seem ready to make concessions. In discussing the content analysis of language, for example, Chapple admits that it may help the 'student of interaction' in his 'understanding of the relations of people'. And even the following statement could be understood to express a viewpoint with which few would disagree, namely, that the study of 'meaning' must go together with the study of actual behaviour and interaction: 'The analysis of symbols must constantly be referred to demonstrable happenings in the interactions of individuals, and these are the only bases for whatever meaning there is to be assigned to the statements of people'.[1] Yet this viewpoint becomes untenable when the 'demonstrable happenings' are reduced to mere interaction rates and frequencies, as in practice they invariably are.

(III) *Small Group Studies*

The last method is essentially an experimental and more sophisticated version of the one just discussed. It was evolved in the Harvard Department of Social Relations in the analysis of small, face-to-face groups, organized for the co-operative performance of given tasks and constituted *ad hoc* for the purpose of the analysis. In the course of the interaction that emerged, definite 'roles' and relationships could be observed to emerge also, though 'role' here means only the gradual fixation of differential behaviour patterns among the co-actors and their acceptance by the group as a whole. In characterizing and measuring these patterns the basic criterion was the contribution of each actor to the total flow of the task-oriented interaction. The contributions

[1] Eliot D. Chapple and Conrad M. Arensberg, 'Measuring Human Relations: An Introduction to the Study of the Interaction of Individuals' (*Genetic Psychology Monographs*, 1940, vol. 22, pp. 108-9).

I

were analysed more specifically in terms of the help, information, reward or censure offered or received by the different actors, their readiness to agree or disagree, and the expressions of emotional stress or relief they introduce into the situation.

The two conditions mentioned above, on which the usefulness of pure interaction studies depends, are both satisfied in this experimental investigation of single-situation, task-oriented groups. More successfully than the method of counting sheer interaction rates, this approach does justice to the varying significance of overt interaction. We may note in passing that this greater success derives from the greater concession made to the qualitative character of the behaviour observed. Even so, this is an analysis under highly artificial conditions, and largely inapplicable to 'real life' situations. Studies of this kind will undoubtedly elucidate the operativeness of roles and relationships in particular situational contexts; but we must not forget that in 'real' situations the roles and relationships have a significant pre-history; they are not created *ex novo* in the contexts in which they are observed to operate. In a sense they are always imported from outside, that is, from the society by whose norms they are decreed and by whose institutions they are fashioned. Furthermore, 'real' roles and relationships are valid for numerous and diverse contexts, so that any overall social structure must be based upon something like the resultant or synthesis of *all* these contexts, each duly weighted according to some criterion of relevance. It is on these grounds that I feel we must reject the more ambitious claims of the students of 'small groups', that their methods are applicable also to the anthropological field and amount to an approach to a true 'social structure'.[1]

5

I now want to suggest my own criteria for that third level abstraction, defining the positional picture of societies. The conditions which such criteria must satisfy have just been stated: they must enable us to synthesize the efficacy of roles and relationships in numerous situations, and must do so on the grounds of some acceptable principle of relevance. I can think

[1] See Robert F. Bales, *Interaction Process Analysis*, 1951.

of two criteria of this kind: (i) The first applies to roles between which there is no 'dissociation', that is, to roles which we know to involve specific relationships with actors in other roles, and which are rendered incomparable only by the qualitative diversity of the relationships. The criterion here is the differential *command over one another's actions*. (ii) The second criterion, though it applies to the first case also, is meant to overcome the 'zones of indeterminacy' in actor-public relationships. In order to do this we reinterpret the 'roles played relative to one another' of individuals so that they have an extraneous reference point; this can be found in the differential *command over existing benefits or resources*.

Employing the first criterion, we have no difficulty in comparing such relationships as father-child, husband-wife, and brother-brother: schematically expressed (using *ca* to indicate 'command over actions')—

(18) $\quad$ Fa (ca) Ch $>$ Hu (ca) Wi $>$ Br (ca) Br

the latter relationship being, for example, such that

$$Br_1 \ (ca) \ Br_2 = Br_2 \ (ca) \ Br_1$$

Identifying 'father' with 'husband' and 'wife' with 'mother', considering brothers on different generation levels, and including various other kinship degrees, we can express the total 'order' of relationships in a chain formula, thus—

(19) $\quad$ Fa (ca) So $>$ Mo (ca) So $>$ Fa (ca) Mo
$\quad\quad$ $<$FaBr (ca) FaBrSo $>$ MoBr (ca) WiSo
$\quad\quad$ $>$FaFa (ca) SoSo $=$ MoFa (ca) FaSo etc.

This is, of course, a fictitious example, though a realistic one. There is nothing very new in the attempt as such to represent systematically a whole order of command relationships; the familiar charts illustrating the 'chain of command' in administrative organizations are based on much the same principle, though they deal with infinitely simpler data. Nor do I claim that one such set of formulae will summarize all the relevant relationships. Equivalent command as, for example, in sibling relationships might have to be expressed separately. We may also need additional symbols, e.g. for zero command, for the peculiar 'negative command' implied in avoidance relationships, and perhaps for command exercised illegitimately. Equally, we must be able to indicate the fluctuating, tug-of-war situation between competitors and rivals, e.g.

(20) $$E\,(ca)\,A \gtreqless A\,(ca)\,E,$$

as well as true conflict relationships, where the actors have incompatible expectations as to their command over one another. Let me leave this last point for the moment and only suggest that, with relatively few additions or changes, sets of formulae of the kind here outlined can give a complete and accurate positional picture. There is only this proviso, which merely repeats a point made already: the picture can be complete or accurate only for a given sector of the society—any sector for which comprehensive role-to-role relationships can at all be constructed.

The positional character of the picture is evidenced by the strictly relational, mathematical symbols ($<, >, =$) which now replace the qualitative signs (a, b, c ... n) of our previous formulae. Let us note also that the new formulae allow for the interlocking of relationships, i.e. for their transitiveness. For if a person E in his particular role stands in relationship to A such that

(21a) $$E\,(ca)\,A,$$

it means that E can also influence and will normally be concerned in any relationships with 'third parties' in which A might be engaged. Thus the formula above can be expanded to

(21b) $$E : (A : T)$$
$$\therefore ErA \rightleftarrows Tr\,(A, E),$$

which is, in transposed form, our crucial formula (17b).[1]

The second criterion permits the direct comparison and interrelation of roles which would otherwise yield only the broad opposition of an actor with his more or less anonymous

---

[1] See p. 87.

'public'. We remember the situation indicated by the diagram below:

Priest ⟶ congregation

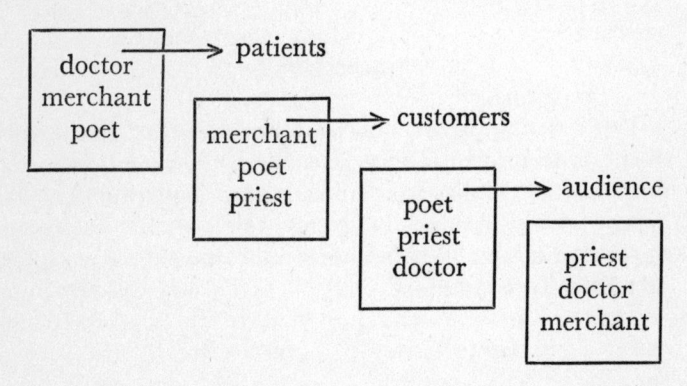

```
┌──────────┐
│ doctor   │⟶ patients
│ merchant │
│ poet     │   ┌──────────┐
└──────────┘   │ merchant │⟶ customers
               │ poet     │
               │ priest   │   ┌──────────┐
               └──────────┘   │ poet     │⟶ audience
                              │ priest   │
                              │ doctor   │   ┌──────────┐
                              └──────────┘   │ priest   │
                                             │ doctor   │
                                             │ merchant │
                                             └──────────┘
```

With the aid of the second criterion each role can be singled out and compared with any other as to their relative 'command over services and benefits' (*crb*); the blanketing collectivities then drop out, being replaced by a series of role-to-role relations for example—

doctor (*crb*) > merchant (*crb*) > priest (*crb*) = poet (*crb*)

If, in this criterion, I am combining existing benefits *and* resources I do so in order to indicate in a single phrase both the gratifications current and favoured in a society and the instrumentalities for their attainment. Differently expressed, the phrase is meant to indicate the possessions and conditions access to which is valued in the society, in a given degree. The employment of the criterion therefore presupposes our ability to construct the appropriate scale of valuation, whether it approximates to the precise 'preference scale' of economists or corresponds to a more abstract and broadly conceived 'scale of worthwhileness', as I have phrased it elsewhere. Yet there is the diversity of the things valued by human beings: which means, in many though not perhaps in all societies, a mingling of scales of valuation similarly diverse and not entirely reducible to one another. Thus we may have to reckon with several discrete value areas or dimensions, or with some combination of them: (i) material resources and benefits; (ii) social dignity (prestige, esteem, status in a hierarchical sense); (iii) cognitive values (learning, knowledge); (iv) emotional, sensual, and æsthetic gratifications; (v) moral values (the fulfilment of duties and 'missions'); and (vi) transcendental values (the 'spiritual' benefits of religion).

This splitting up of *crb* does not however weaken the efficiency of the criterion; in a sense it enhances it since it permits us to demonstrate significant interrelations between the different types of this command. Let $>$ and $<$ now stand for greater and lesser command; then societies may be characterized by the fact that, for example,

$$(22) \qquad crb \ (i) \ > \ \rightleftarrows \ crb \ (vi) \ <, \text{ or}$$
$$ \qquad crb \ (i) \ > \ \rightleftarrows \ crb \ (ii) \ >.$$

The first formula would apply to societies which believe in the spiritual value of poverty; the second, to the many societies where wealth means prominence.

Obviously, like the command over the actions of others, the command over resources and benefits implies the possibility of conflict, when people, in virtue of their roles, have incompatible expectations or make incompatible claims concerning their access to the existing desiderata. But the two criteria are altogether closely related and even overlap. Command over resources will clearly often lead to command over the actions of others. The latter, in turn, is one of the instrumentalities for the attainment of material benefits, the benefits of 'social dignity', and perhaps others as well. Also, command over other people's actions may itself be considered a 'benefit' (as when 'power' is considered desirable for its own sake), additional to if not coinciding with the other instances of 'social dignity'.

The link between this value area and the command over the actions of others is even closer. For the benefits exemplified by prestige or esteem, as they are attainable through command over the actions of others, also imply a measure of this command by definition. As suggested before, having prestige, gaining the esteem or enjoying the deference of others, already means being able to command their actions in some respect. Symbolically expressed—

(23) $$ca \longrightarrow crb \text{ (ii)} \supset ca$$

This formula, incidentally, represents a true sociological 'law'; for the circularity expressed in it is a fundamental aspect of prestige and similar states of social dignity, which may always be both sources of command and consequences of it (as when a man with a large following gains prestige for this reason, and can then count on further people offering their deference). In this sense the command over the actions of others is cumulative, through leading to some form of social dignity and expanding in virtue of it.

The interrelation between the two command criteria has a further significance, more germane to the issue under discussion. The second criterion might seem to belong to the purely distributive level of structure, merely demonstrating the way in which benefits or access to them are allocated to the various classes of people making up the society. But this is not so. Since such access always has something to do with the command people exercise over one another, it is also to that extent evidence of interactive alignments. Let me put it this way: it is because other people facilitate or hinder my attainment of certain commonly valued benefits that I in fact attain them in such-and-such measure. More generally speaking, it is in consequence of all the possible relationships between actors that each actor also receives his allocation of benefits: so that the measure of this allocation also synthesizes numerous, perhaps all, interactive relationships and demonstrates their interlocking. Somewhat modified, our formula (17b) once more lends itself to defining the situation; replacing the symbol for the 'third' actor (T) by the sign indicating command over resources and benefits, great or less great, we can write:

(24) if $E : A [\gtrless (crb)]$ is such that
$ErA \supset E (ca) A$
$\therefore ErA \longrightarrow A [\gtrless (crb)].$

It is important to stress that this dependence of *crb* upon all the *ca* relationships in which a person is involved is not reversible. Although one's command over resources and benefits is likely to lead to some command over the actions of others, it need not do so with regard to all the persons with whom one comes in contact. A high degree of *crb* (i), especially, may well go together with low or zero *ca* towards certain people, that is, with unassuming, familiar, or 'democratic' behaviour. This means that certain relationships can properly be described only by combining the two criteria. And this, in turn, has far-reaching consequences. For if we use both criteria together we can let one (*crb*) represent the role typified by it and employ the other to indicate the relationships in which the actors so described are involved. The actors then become simply anonymous persons—any person in any role characterized by the given degree of *crb*: while the *ca* relationship will characterize their command over other persons similarly anonymous. It will be seen that by this method we can carry abstraction to a point where even the last element of 'quality' disappears—roles described as such. In other words, we are finally able to deal purely with 'positions', and we are able to do so without being trapped by tautologies.

As for the practical advantage of this method of exposition, it renders structural descriptions infinitely transposable. Let me illustrate this with the help of our earlier paradigm, the juxtaposition, in many kinship systems, of two complementary relationships, one disciplinarian, the other friendly; as we suggested at the time, the same principle may well apply also to widely different situations, e.g. in politics or business (see pp. 105f.). To demonstrate this wider validity means, in concrete terms, to find a general proposition covering all the following cases: a father who is a 'friend' while the mother's brother is the 'disciplinarian'; a father who is a disciplinarian while the grandfather is the friend; a political leader whose authoritarian position is balanced by that of a 'people's tribune'—a man still of leadership status but on familiar and equal terms with the subjects; and a strict 'boss', assisted by a more approachable deputy or 'public relations man'. Let me restate the positional picture common to all these situations: it lies in the fact that a superiority rigidly exercised goes together with a superiority softened and minimized. Put in yet another way, we have a triad involving two persons in 'superior' roles, one of whom acts authoritatively towards the subordinates, the other, in a friendly and more egalitarian fashion.

The superiority in question, whether it derives from kinship position, leadership status, or rank in the business organization, inevitably implies a relatively great crb (i or ii). Let crb therefore stand for all the roles so characterized; and let ca stand for the behaviour evinced by the actors, authoritarian or friendly. The common positional picture is then characterized by this proposition: if two persons (in whatever roles) are so related that

(25a) $\qquad$ A $(crb) \gg$ E (crb), and
$\qquad\qquad$ A (ca) E $\gg$ E (ca) A,

there is a third person T such that

(25b) $\qquad$ T $(crb) >$ A (crb), yet (approximately)
$\qquad\qquad$ T (ca) A $=$ A (ca) T.

If the proposition as here stated really holds, it amounts to a general social regularity or 'law'. Whether or not it does hold, is an empirical question, and beyond this context. What is important in the present context is that the very expression of the law would depend on the employment of the two criteria of command.

6

These, however, could be criticised on other grounds. It might, for example, be objected that I have taken it for granted too readily that we can in fact accurately locate, identify and measure the two kinds of command. But if I have taken it for granted, I have done no more than affirm a familiar competence of social enquiry. Though it may still be in need of considerable refinement, we constantly exercise it; that is, we freely rank values and notions of 'worthwhileness' and operate with such concepts as power, authority, or hierarchical status, assessing their magnitudes; which is precisely what we are doing when applying the criteria of command. And if, in view of this, it is argued that the 'social structure' I am envisaging is little more than a power, authority or status structure, I would reply that this seems to me the only 'dimension' both sufficiently abstract for our purpose and still sufficiently relevant, in the sense of being important in human and social existence. Let me make it clear that in saying this I do not wish to suggest anything in the way of universal human motivations or desires inherent in 'human nature'. I am making no assumptions whatever about people's love of command or thirst for power, and I have not argued in the way I did because I believe that it is 'necessary and justifiable to assume that a conscious or unconscious wish to gain power is a very general motive in human affairs.'[1] All that it is 'necessary and justifiable' for us to accept is a certain degree of abstraction, and the fact that command relationships exemplify it most satisfactorily.

The two criteria yield these or similar descriptive categories: The first—dominance, submission, equality; superordination, subordination, co-ordination; symmetry and asymmetry in relations; and onesided or reciprocal dependence. The second—superiority, inferiority, equality; and degrees of access and entitlement, with the limiting values of complete inclusion or exclusion. Each set of categories could be translated into the appropriate formulae, though this is too obvious to need illustration. Nor are the categories themselves in any way new or unfamiliar. Significantly, they are used in much the same sense as names for relationships seen structurally, in the 'pure' or 'formal' sociology of Simmel and von Wiese.[2] Are they too 'pure' and 'formal', too empty of context and hence uninformative? The answer is that this rigorous formalism, and the consequent 'emptiness' of the description, are the price we must pay for the extraction of an embracing and strictly positional picture of societies. Whether or not this is too great a price we may for the moment leave undecided.

This is not denying that, in practice, it is rarely feasible to exclude descriptions in qualitative terms altogether, even from the most consistent structural analysis. How far this intrusion or concession should go is a question of usefulness and convenience, on which there are no firm rules. There are, however, two ele-

---

[1] E. R. Leach, *Political Systems in Highland Burma*, p. 10.
[2] *The Sociology of Georg Simmel*, ed. K. H. Wolff, part III; L. von Wiese, *System der Allgemeinen Soziologie*, 1933, vol. I, pp. 205, 216-77.

ments or aspects of human relationships the omission of which would seriously impair any social analysis. The first is their emotionally *loaded* or *neutral* character; the second, the actors' expectations as to the *retention* or *relinquishment* of the relationships.[1] The two aspects clearly hang together; we know enough about human relationships to predict that their expected retention will tend to involve some emotional bond (or 'sentiment'), and the anticipation of their change, some strain or perhaps hostility. The two aspects are, however, of a logically different order. For the emotional loading of relationships is merely one of the qualitative features which a rigorous abstraction might ignore or 'bracket away', and which we now suggest should be 'put back'; while the retention or relinquishment of relationships bears on an element in the structure itself, namely, its dynamic properties. This is a new problem, not so far considered, to which we shall return in a different context.

It is hardly necessary to stress, in conclusion, that the positional criteria here developed apply to the 'external' order of groups no less than to their 'internal' order, that is, to the relationships between sub-groups of the society no less than to the relationships between actors or persons. The former exhibits the same positional possibilities—superordination, subordination, coordination, dominance and equality, inclusion in and exclusion from benefits and resources, etc. We need only remember that, here as elsewhere, the interrelation of sub-groups basically rests on the actions of individuals—now individuals exercising the given command or access in a representative capacity, in virtue of corporate entitlements vested in their groups.

It follows that there need be no congruence between the position of actors when enacting their roles within their groups and their position when acting in their corporate capacity *vis-à-vis* or relative to other groups. Sub-groups which have a

---

[1] The emotionally loaded or neutral character of relationships corresponds to the first of the five 'basic pattern variables' determining the character of social actions in Parsons's theoretical system (there called 'affectivity—affective neutrality'). The categories 'retention' and 'relinquishment' appear as the two basic possibilities in the 'primary mechanisms of adjustment'. (See Talcott Parsons and Edward Shils, *Toward a General Theory of Action*, 1951, pp. 77, 256.) The analogy, however, does not go beyond this very general correspondence.

hierarchical internal structure may be equivalent within the society at large (e.g. parallel descent groups or segments, each with its different command position derived from descent-cum-age); or the internal hierarchical structure may be cancelled by the external one (e.g. when leadership or seniority in a low caste group is compared with inferior position in a high caste group); or finally, the equivalence of roles in a sub-group may go together with a hierarchical ordering of that sub-group in the wider society (as when an egalitarian association or religious sect is placed high or low among other associations or sects).

These are all straightforward issues, which involve no new problems. It is, in fact, easy to see that our three instances of incongruence between the internal and external order of sub-groups are the only possible ones, and that they can be directly deduced from the conjunction of the two principles, the dichotomization of roles, and the progressive abstraction of relationships to mere command differentials.

With this, we have completed the main part of our analysis. Having reached the end of this 'progress in abstraction', we have also reached the end of our progress towards a strictly positional picture of the society or, which means the same, towards social structure rigorously understood. It now remains to evaluate the results.

VI

STRUCTURE, TIME AND REALITY

In evaluating structural as against any other type of social analysis two claims are usually made: first, that structural analysis lends to the social data a higher degree of comparability;[1] and second, that it renders them more readily quantifiable.[2] Both claims are borne out by the approach here developed. In as much as it implies the abstraction of the relatively invariant features of social situations—roles and their interrelation—it enhances the comparability of the social situations themselves. It is for the same reason, incidentally, that the concept of structure assumes its fundamental importance in logic: there, too, comparability (without which there could be no systematizing of anything) is considered to rest on 'relation likeness', i.e. on structure.[3] And in as much as in this process of abstraction we progressively leave behind (or 'bracket away') the qualitative characteristics of social situations—the aims, needs, ideas, and emotions bound up in human behaviour—we should also be able to present our data in quantifiable form.

No one is likely to deny that the satisfactory quantification of anthropological data still presents serious methodological difficulties. Admittedly, we have made considerable progress in this respect, to wit the numerous statistics of various kinds which we now compile almost as a matter of course, concerning marriage, residence patterns, social mobility, household budgets, the size of kin groups, their fission and accretion, and so forth. But these are all aspects of social life which it is easy to quantify since they themselves represent quantities, magnitudes or frequency

[1] See A. R. Radcliffe-Brown, 'On Social Structure', *J.R.A.I.*, 1940, vol. LXX, p. 5; E. E. Evans-Pritchard, *Social Anthropology*, 1951, p. 18; Fred Eggan, *Social Organization of the Western Pueblos*, 1950, p. 9.
[2] See M. Fortes, 'Time and Social Structure', in *Social Structure: Studies presented to A. R. Radcliffe-Brown*, 1949, p. 57.
[3] Susan Stebbing, *A Modern Introduction to Logic*, p. 205.

rates, or are at least directly translatable into this order of facts. Many others, possibly of greater relevance, permit measurement only by indirect and much more precarious methods, involving the interpretation of signs and the discovery of indices of some kind. It is in this sense that we look for indices of social esteem or deference, for signs indicating the strength of beliefs, loyalties or 'sentiments', or for any pointers to the stability of relationships and the like. There is no need to pursue this point further.[1] All we need say is that our two criteria of social structure are at least partly of this kind. Involving as they do degrees of command, they are also basically quantitative concepts; but their precise translation into magnitudes and measures is as yet far from unproblematic.

At the same time, even though adequate quantification may at the moment be difficult, we can at least employ a related procedure, that of geometrization. That is to say, we can operate with non-metric social models—with diagrams, blueprints, charts, maps, and similar illustrative devices. This, too, has been mentioned as one of the advantages of structural analysis.[2] And if geometrization is not a full substitute for quantification it yet suggests this final value of the concern with social structure: that it enables us to present our data neatly, synoptically, and with some elegance.

Yet precisely this possibility seems to indicate also a serious weakness or incompleteness of structural analysis. For the greater the facility with which it can employ geometrical, spatial models, the less, it seems, must be its capacity to take account of events *in time* affecting and varying the social structure. I hope to show that this apparent weakness rests on a misunderstanding; and I shall in this connection deal with two further misunderstandings often met with in discussions about structure— the tendency to reify the concept, and the all-too-sweeping distinction of structure and function. The last question will most conveniently be dealt with somewhat out of order, towards the end of this discussion.

---

[1] See my essay 'Understanding Primitive Peoples' (*Oceania*, 1956, vol. XXVI, pp. 159-173).
[2] See John W. Bennet and Melvin M. Tumin, *Social Life*, 1948, p. 70; G. A. Lundberg, *Social Research*, pp. 326 ff.

Let us make this general point first. In the interest of accuracy we should keep apart the two things, the social structure defined by our two command criteria, being the highly refined end product of structural analysis as we understand the procedure, and the analytical procedure itself; and a little later I shall try to evaluate the two separately. At the moment I propose to deal with them together. Which means that in discussing the properties of social structure bearing on time, reality, and function I shall be discussing their place not only in the final positional picture, but in the whole approach that enables us to construct it, including results obtained as it were mid-way, on lower levels of abstraction. There is nothing peculiar or dubious about this. If you wish to test the correctness or power of some mathematical formula you will obviously test also, by implication if not specifically, the whole method of calculation that led up to it. So much by way of introduction.

2

Now the first 'test' concerns what various scholars seem to regard as the blind spot of structural analysis—its inability to cope with the time dimension. The generally 'synchronic' approach of modern social anthropology may contribute towards this weakness. But it could be argued that the concern with social structure imposes it, since the very concept implies invariant relations, the abstraction of a positional order, and hence a static treatment of social reality. In presenting our positional picture we do not perhaps freeze an ongoing course of events at some arbitrary point; but we try to extract from it an orderliness assumed to be continuous and persistent, that is, to have a relatively timeless validity. Firth has made this point most sharply when he contends that social structure expresses the 'continuity' of social life, its persistence and invariance, and no more: so that we need another, complementary concept, *organization*, in which 'time enters', in order to do justice to variance and change and to the many 'acts of choice and decision' underlying these effects.[1] This viewpoint has some similarity with that of economists, when they distinguish

[1] *Elements of Social Organization*, pp. 39-40.

'static analysis', concerned with the position obtaining at a given time, from 'dynamic analysis', which considers the 'decisions' that led to the given position or may affect future ones.[1] I wish to argue against this equation of structural with static analysis and against certain misunderstandings that lead to it. In essence, I want to suggest that the whole problem of finding a corrective for this alleged 'blind spot' of structural analysis does not in fact exist.

To begin with a very trivial point: this problem would exist if the concept of structure *ex definitione* excluded recognition of events and processes in time. This is obviously not so; among the possible relations which cause us to ascribe 'structure' to phenomena is also succession in time, an interrelation of parts defined by the criteria of 'earlier' and 'later', as in a sentence or pieces of music.[2] Now I do not suggest that social structure is of this simple kind; indeed, its temporal implications are vastly more complicated, and I shall presently indicate some of them. Nor do I deny that, when we analyse social structure (the positions of actors relative to one another, the 'network' of their relationships), we do use language suggestive of, and suitable for, static states, *as if* the positions were fixed and timeless, and the relationships simply continuous. But let us be clear that this is only '*as-if*' language. For we cannot but define social positions in terms of behaviour sequences, which consume time and happen on a time scale; relationships cannot but be abstracted from successive, repetitive actions (Firth's 'acts of choice and decision'), which we collect together in such class concepts as subordination, reciprocity, respect, loyalty, rivalry, and the like. Time 'enters' in all of these. If our descriptive categories do not refer to the time factor more explicitly, we yet imply it, much as we may say of two seaports that 'they *are* linked by boat', meaning, of course, that boats move between them more or less regularly.

In brief, the terms 'invariance' or 'continuity' in fact refer to recurrence and repetitiveness. Social structure, as Fortes once put it, must be 'visualized' as 'a sum of processes in time'.[3] As I would phrase it, social structure is implicitly an event-structure;

---

[1] Joseph A. Schumpeter, *History of Economic Analysis*, 1954, p. 963.
[2] Bertrand Russell, *Human Knowledge: Its Scope and Limits*, 1948, p. 272.
[3] *The Web of Kinship among the Tallensi*, 1949, p. 342.

and if we describe it in quasi-static terms it is because we wish to demonstrate the 'uniformities' in the 'underlying processes' and because their 'constancy within certain limits . . . is a workable assumption'.[1] A better analogy than the example of the boats and seaports is probably the analysis, in physics, of molecular structure. Though this analysis again reveals only event series—the movements of particles in time—their regularity can be represented in quasi-continuous 'pathways' or 'orbits'. I do not think that I am stretching the analogy too far when I compare social relationships with such 'pathways' or 'orbits', discernable, in the social field, in the repetitive behavioural events.

In two respects, moreover, the time dimension is not only implicit in the social structure, but constitutes an explicit condition of it. Both have to do with the recruitment of people into roles, relationships, and groups so-and-so structured, that is, with the mechanics of intake and circulation. These too must be explicitly defined, lest we describe positions without indicating how they are filled; and once we indicate this, we also indicate processes in the full sense of the word, with 'earlier' and 'later' stages, and composed of phases and timed pocedures. But the two special instances I have in mind refer not only to a mere redistribution of the population, but to the redistribution, the displacement and replacement, of the roles and relationships they fill.

The first concerns roles or positions which cannot be defined save in dynamic terms, i.e. in terms indicating movement and positional change. I mentioned before the expectations of actors regarding the retention or relinquishment of their roles. There clearly exist a great many roles in which the expectation of relinquishment is a regular feature, and many relationships rendered discontinuous or unstable for this reason. The 'child' who will grow up; the 'novice' who outgrows the novitiate; the 'cross-cousin' who becomes a potential spouse and the 'bride' who becomes a wife; the 'immigrant' who becomes a citizen and the man awaiting promotion (or fearing demotion): they all play roles and are involved in relationships the very definition of which requires the reference to the progress or passing of time. In a sense, this type of role is complementary to the

[1] Talcott Parsons, *Essays in Sociological Theory*, p. 22.

'developing' or 'unfolding' roles, envisaged as being built up in the course of time (see pp. 38, 43). If in one case one plays or begins to play a role so that its full assumption and retention may follow, in the other one is expected to play it so that it may in due course be relinquished and exchanged. We may note also a possible overlap with the summation of roles, when the 're-linquishment' is not intended to be complete. To the extent to which it is meant to be effective, the roles and relationships in question are *self-liquidating:* the actors (and their society) conceive of them as lasting only for a given time, whether this is predictable or not, and as precursory to some other role or relationship, conceivably one entailing a greater command over benefits and the actions of others. Needless to say, groups and societies differ in the scope they afford to these periodical shifts, and the orderliness of any social system will be characterized by the measure of self-liquidation it allows or promotes. Equally, the self-liquidation may involve whole groups and all roles within it, such as some of the 'feeder groups' touched on before, or the 'impermanent' family as compared with the permanent lineage, age grades as against age sets, etc.

The second instance is exemplified in all conflict relationships, which similarly require the reference to progress in time, to some anticipated shift or readjustment, and to a measure of self-liquidation. It is convenient, and I think basically correct, to extend the meaning of 'conflict' so as to include also the forms of antagonism we normally call competition and rivalry. Now as I suggested earlier, any conflict relationship can be broken down to the incompatible expectations of actors in their roles in regard to their command over existing benefits or over one another. Thus, if two actors (E and A) understand their roles to be such that

$$\text{for E} \ldots \text{E} \ (ca) \ A > A \ (ca) \ E$$
$$\text{for A} \ldots \text{E} \ (ca) \ A < A \ (ca) \ E, \text{ or}$$
$$\text{for E} \ldots \text{E} \ (crb) > A \ (crb)$$
$$\text{for A} \ldots \text{E} \ (crb) < A \ (crb),$$

then the relationship between them does not 'look the same' from each actor's viewpoint; its two forms cease to be equivalent and hence indicate conflict:

$$E r A \not\equiv A r E.$$

Logically, this is the same formula we previously derived from interaction situations in which the actors have incongruent conceptions of each other's roles (see pp. 52f.). In suggesting, however, that all conflict relationships are thus reducible to incompatible or incongruent role conceptions I have oversimplified the position a little. It hardly needs restating that we are, as a matter of course, concerned not with idiosyncratic, purely 'personal' conflicts, but with conflicts in some measure determined or engendered by the institutional make-up of the society, that is, with conflicts in which people become involved in virtue of the obtaining rights and obligations (or roles). Such conflicts are thoroughly familiar, whether they refer to roles so conceived that they involve irreconcilable claims (a husband's rights over his wife as against her obligations towards her own kin) or to roles sufficiently ambiguous for the actors to interpret them differently (as when the nobility by descent consider themselves superior to persons of wealth, who may reject this claim). In either case the conflict is intrinsic as it were to the pre-existing roles.

But individuals may be involved in conflicts while, at that time, playing no role foreshadowing them: as when a man, in whatever role, becomes the lover of a married woman and hence a rival of her husband, when people quarrel and become enemies, or when someone comes to challenge established authority. Though the origin of the conflict may thus be merely fortuitous and idiosyncratic, it will be conventionalized or 'routinized' in the sense that more or less precise roles exist which fit these particular conditions ('paramour', 'enemy', 'rebel'). Strictly speaking, then, the conflict does not ensue in consequence of the roles, though once it arises it carries the given role with it, with all its 'further' implications of expected conduct and responses to it.

Whichever way the conflict is engendered, by the character of the roles themselves or by the drift of pre-role behaviour, the relationships embodying it bear explicitly on progress in time. Either they lead to a typically fluctuating, tug-of-war-like situation, characterized by repetitive acts of competition or opposition; or they move towards an eventual resolution brought about by the relinquishment of one or both of the opposed roles, in the form of victory, defeat, or simply withdrawal from the conflict. Though we have been speaking of dyadic relationships only, the same also holds for whole classes and collectivities of persons involved in rivalry, competition and conflict. The enduring 'balanced opposition' of groups often mentioned by anthropologists is probably only a variant of the tug-of-war situation, when neither side has the chance or is expected to try the decisive pull. In each case the conflict relationship is conceived of as progressing from the obtaining command relationship to a future one, even though each shift may only be a step towards a further shift, and the self-liquidation of the roles and relationships might be indefinitely suspended.

True it is that, once we allow in this fashion for the time dimension, we also allow for a certain amount of discontinuity and instability in roles, relationships, and whole clusters of them. But the roles and relationships which are thus being surrendered and exchanged of course continue to exist, though enacted by an ever-varying personnel and hence filled discontinuously. On occasion, there may be a real hiatus, as when a community is temporarily without 'brides', 'novices', 'leaders' or persons competing for some position. Yet the roles and relationships missing at one moment will be back at the next, since they belong to the permanent repertory of societies. Conversely, there may be two sets of relationships at one moment where previously there was only one, as when kin groups undergo fission. Even so, both the relationships and the possibility of their duplication belong to the 'permanent repertory'. We might say that roles and relationships are being constantly redistributed through the population; or we might say that people move in and out of roles and relationships, so that these too go and come, cease and begin again. Whichever way we look at it, the sequences of events involved are infinitely repetitive through the society, reproducing broadly identical configurations of elements (actors in relationships, relationships interlocking), something that can be put on an unchanging map. In this sense they still indicate overall invariance and 'workable constancy'. Thus, in spite of the explicit admission of the time dimension we are still entitled to speak of structure. We need only concede that it has dynamic properties, containing within it the internal shifts and fluctuations that go with displacement and replacement. If we employed our old simile of a network—an 'as-if' network, to be sure—we should have to admit that its knots keep on being tied and retied and that parts of it all the time disappear and reappear: but when the knots are being retied and the strands reappear, this happens as it were in the old places. The picture as a whole remains more or less the same. In other words, we are still able to draw up diagrams and blueprints, though they will have to include symbols indicating 'directed movement' (or 'vectors') as well as positions apparently at rest, and though our 'pathways' or 'orbits' will have to allow for jumps from one to the other.

If I have used illustrations and metaphors rather profusely I have done so because we do not seem to have ready, simple terms to describe this combination of internal redistributions and overall invariance. I am reluctant to resort to such shadowy phrases as 'dynamic equilibrium' or 'boundary maintaining system' (Parsons). I am reluctant, too, to adopt Radcliffe-Brown's distinction between *social structure* as such, as 'the set of actually existing relations, at a given moment of time' and linking 'certain human beings', and *structural form*, which 'remains relatively constant over a larger or shorter period of time' and links together 'social persons'.[1] For relations of the former kind cannot be credited with invariance, without which condition we cannot intelligently talk about structure at all. Nor would I speak of 'rearrangements' in the sense in which Radcliffe-Brown calls every marriage 'essentially a rearrangement of the social structure'.[2] For what is being rearranged in this and similar cases is not the general orderliness (or 'system') of the relationships existing in the society, but merely particular relationships, involving particular people at particular times: this is still an instance of intake and of the self-liquidation (as well as summation) of roles with the consequent internal shifts.

But we can, I think, profitably borrow the economists' concept of *stationary states*. In its least rigorous (not 'thoroughgoing') form, the stationary state is understood to include precisely the internal shifts and fluctuations with which we are concerned,

---

[1] *Structure and Function in Primitive Society*, p. 192.
[2] *African Systems of Kinship and Marriage*, p. 43.

produced by the appearance and disappearance of elements and by the forming and re-forming of interrelations. It is stationary only in the sense that 'displacements' are 'offset by replacements' and that the two are 'equal on the whole'.[1] To some extent, as we know, social structures, in their distributive aspects, include precise numerical constancies of this kind, concerning particular roles, occupations, offices, or the formation of sub-groups (see above, p. 17). But even if they do not, and if any precise 'offsets' are precluded by the vagaries of demographic factors and other uncontrollable fluctuations, the model of stationary states seems sufficiently elastic to accommodate also this more fluid state of affairs. At the moment we cannot really assess the degree of this fluidity since, in anthropology, this field is virtually unexplored. Nobody has counted or is likely to count roles, relationships, and every kind of sub-group from moment to moment. Let us then say, very broadly, that structural analysis presents societies as if they were in stationary states. Just how large is the share of the 'as if', we shall presently discuss further. There is no need to stress again that the analysis itself is neither static nor insensitive to time; which distinction, incidentally, between a method involving 'dynamic' considerations (or 'models') and the stationary processes described by it, is once more in accord with economic theory.[2]

3

So much for the role of the time dimension in structural analysis. Firth's argument, however, from which we started, demands further consideration. In dealing with the problem of time he in essence deals with the problem of change and with the 'dilemma' with which the latter presents the student of social structure. The dilemma is simply this, that 'a structural analysis alone cannot interpret social change', while living societies always combine structure and change. All societies, as Firth points out, provide for the 'systematic ordering of social relations by acts of choice and decision'. Though people would look to 'structure' as to a 'reliable guide to actions', they also

[1] A. C. Pigou, *The Economics of Stationary States*, 1935, pp. 8-9.
[2] Joseph A. Schumpeter, op. cit. p. 964; P. A. Samuelson, *Foundations of Economic Analysis*, 1948, p. 262.

take decisions which 'may affect the future structural alignment'. Again, only the concept of organization, not of structure, can express these instances of 'variance and change'.[1]

Here it seems useful to introduce the distinction recently drawn by Lévi-Strauss between *micro-time* and *macro-time*. Lévi-Strauss does little more than suggest these two concepts, exemplifying the first by the data produced by sociometry and by Levin's kindred method of social topology, and the second, by the happenings and trends of history.[2] But I think that I interpret Lévi-Strauss correctly when I apply the two concepts to the situation here discussed, in this sense: Micro-time provides the time scale for events described a moment ago, that is, for the shifts, movements and variations which still remain within the bounds of some overall constancy; conversely, macro-time contains the kinds of events which, in Firth's phrase, change the pre-existing 'structural alignment'. In a word, events in micro-time do not invalidate a structural schema, while events in macro-time may do so.

Now it is obvious that if any individual act or series of acts does indeed permanently alter the pre-existing structural alignment, this change itself can no longer be represented in the same structural schema. Repetitiveness would simply cease, and we could no longer abstract any invariant order or positional picture. That such changes happen is of course beyond doubt, whether they do so gradually, in consequence of cumulative departures from the norm, or more or less suddenly, as the result of revolutions and similar upheavals. It obviously makes sense to say that a matrilineal kinship system has given way to a patrilineal one, that rigid castes have been replaced by more fluid social classes, or (to quote a famous example) that the social structure appropriate to feudalism turned into the kind of structure entailed in capitalism. But there is nothing puzzling about the notion that a particular social structure as described at a certain moment may only be accurate for a particular period of time. It may not be easy to say precisely when the picture ceases to be accurate; also, at some stage in the transition it may be too confused altogether, lacking the constancies needed

[1] Op. cit. pp. 35, 40.
[2] In *Anthropology Today*, ed. A. L. Kroeber, p. 532.

for the extraction of any 'ordered arrangement'. But the fact that the transformation does occur presents no logical difficulties. In brief, the structural realignments on a macro-time scale are unproblematic.

But Firth's argument concerns more complicated and more subtle issues. The 'decisions and choices' he has in mind are much more diffuse than these massive social transformations; they effect not any total shift, but move-by-move rearrangements, and they happen all the time, in the manner of readjustments to never-quite-identical circumstances. More precisely, Firth's argument concerns the latitude allowed to actors in interpreting their roles and managing their relations with one another. This implies an undoubted fact, that individuals, at various stages of their lives, face options, such as those involved in the selection of a spouse, in the coexistence of virilocal and uxorilocal residence, in the choice of occupations and of political allegiance, and many others. Societies may be so rigidly organized that these options are reduced to a minimum, conduct being widely predetermined by some unvarying routine. In so far as such options exist, the individual has no unequivocal routine to guide him and relieve him of decision. But let us be clear that the decision is rarely an entirely novel one, taken without any guiding model or precedent. Usually, the different options are themselves part of the social routine, if an ambiguous one, and precedents or models exemplifying one or the other step, with all its consequences, surround one on all sides. For the individual, the choice and decision he has to make will indeed affect the future 'alignment' in which he (and others) will be placed. But from the observer's point of view the choices and decisions, if they still derive from an established routine, will yet be demonstrable in terms of a prevailing and continuous overall orderliness, even though this will be complicated by parallel or alternative possibilities.

It is obvious that there always is a first time when such decisions are made and become precedents for the subsequent regularized options, though our empirical evidence will rarely lead us to it. It is possible, further, that over a period of time the sequence of individual options may be such that their relative frequency undergoes a definite, perhaps progressive, change.

In other words, the move-by-move variances will add up to a final total shift. For example, a type of marriage once preferential gradually ceases to be so; virilocal and uxorilocal residence, evenly balanced at one stage, will appear unevenly balanced at another; certain occupations will expand while others will contract, or the established political authorities will lose effective command. In such events the prevailing orderliness will also be objectively altered. And it seems justifiable, in view of this possibility, to ascribe to each individual choice and decision, novel or no, the potential capacity of affecting the 'future structural alignment'. But disregarding such contingencies for the moment and considering only the move-by-move availability of options and alternatives, it is, I think a mistaken view to regard it as beyond the grasp of structural analysis. If variance of this kind is in fact ignored or misrepresented, this is due not to any inherent limitations of the concept of structure, but to its ambiguous handling.

To begin with, structural analysis does lend itself to oversimplification in the sense that we are apt to concentrate on averages or typical situations. If, for example we find that in a certain primitive society patrilineal descent counts in most spheres of life and on all 'normal' occasions, while the matrilineal link (or 'option') is effective only in limited contexts or in the case of individuals in special positions, we are easily tempted to speak summarily of a 'patrilineal' structure. The exceptions are, though not ignored, yet relegated to the background. But a careful analysis would refer to these variations as explicitly as to the 'average'; it would demonstrate the contexts and conditions in which one or the other principle comes into play, and may well express the relation between what appear to be 'normal' and 'exceptional' circumstances in quantitative and statistical terms. Thus, when analysing the kinship structure of the Nupe I have used the phrase 'second line of defence' to indicate the particular character of matrilineal options in a patrilineal system;[1] more recently Fortes carried out a brilliant analysis, on a statistical basis, of the delicate balance between patrilocal and matrilocal factors in the Ashanti kinship system. With Fortes we must agree on the 'futility', in instances like

[1] *A Black Byzantium*, 1942, p. 32.

these, of summary description like 'patrilocality' or matrilocality'.[1] But we must go further and say that studies which exhibit some statistical scatter of the relevant features, that is, which exhibit 'degrees of freedom' or 'latitude' in choices and decisions, are still studies of structure. In brief, structure and variance (within limits) are not inherently contradictory; rather the former is defined or built up through taking account of the latter. When the scatter is large and the variance goes considerably beyond simple alternatives, the resulting situation becomes exceedingly difficult to describe. In fact, we may not at the moment possess satisfactory techniques to represent and characterize such 'multivariant' structures. But let us be clear that this is a deficiency of our symbolic devices, our nomenclature, two-dimensional diagrams, and so forth, not of the conceptual tool we are using.

Let me insert this observation. If the variance is unlimited, if there is no routine guiding people's options so that these have a random scatter, then we can extract no orderliness or structure from the situation so characterized. Whether such amorphous situations are likely to occur in reality, save in some narrow sector of society or in a transitional, thoroughly disturbed (or 'anomic') phase, is irrelevant. We can envisage approximations to it, for example, a fully bilateral descent system in which none of the possible affiliations is 'discarded' and each represents an equal option. Needless to say, such systems do not exist, since there is always some 'limitation' of the possibilities, by exclusion or, we should add, by a grading of the options.[2] But there is an interesting point of theory involved in this. If the options were really unlimited and exhibited a random scatter, this would mean that every conceivable choice would be made in equal proportion (at least over a period). Assume, then, that we find all the possible attitudes, say, of fathers to sons (disciplinarian, friendly, disinterested, indulgent, etc.) thus equally represented in our sample, whether it concerns the numbers of fathers and sons at a given moment or their behaviour over time. Clearly, this kind of relationship is indeterminate and can no longer be

---

[1] 'Time and Social Structure', in *Social Structure: Studies presented to A. R. Radcliffe-Brown*, 1949, p. 83.
[2] G. P. Murdock, *Social Structure*, 1949, p. 44.

defined, as little as roles can be defined which consist entirely of optional attributes. Consequently, this particular sector of social life ceases to be demonstrable as part of the social structure. Yet this conclusion does not always apply. It does not apply to limited options, even if they are made in equal proportions. We should certainly not consider the situation amorphous or unstructured if, in a given society, the choices between virilocal and uxorilocal residence or patrilineal and matrilineal affiliation are by and large equal. On the contrary, we should take the balance itself to be a relevant structural feature.

The answer, in general terms, seems to be this. It is not enough to say as we did a moment ago, that structure and variance within limits can go together. We must add that social structure, to be definable, requires a *gradient* in the possible variance of behaviour. In other words, some options must be preferred to others. There are two possibilities. The options offered by the social routine may be limited, perhaps to evenly balanced choices: in which case the gradient is between the choices actually offered (and made) and all the other theoretically possible ones (which have zero preference). Or the permitted options are (roughly) unlimited, i.e. they approximate to the number of theoretically possible choices: then there must still be a routine grading their preference. For example, the numerous varying attitudes of fathers to sons must fall, say, on a curve of 'normal distribution'. The possibility of unlimited variance is theoretically interesting also in another respect; for it proves that the dependence of structure on stationary states is not reversible. The continued reproduction of randomly distributed options has clearly stationary effects; but it does not amount to structure, in the sense just explained.

The presupposition of stationary states or constancies in general presents a further, methodologically more important problem. Structure, inasmuch as it implies relative (or 'workable') constancy, is capable of being expressed in norms. But being abstracted from numerous observational data, this kind of norm is primarily empirical and statistical. It is not necessarily valid for the people we observe; it is not, as it were, a 'real thing', a state of affairs which the people actively seek or uphold. At the same time some such ordered arrangement as we perceive in the society (and call 'structure') will also be perceived by the people and recognized or envisaged as a set of norms governing conduct. Fred Eggan makes a similar point.[1] And Lévi-Strauss suggestively speaks of the 'lived-in orders' of societies, which can be 'studied from outside and as part of objective reality', as against their 'thought-of orders', on which societies rely 'to achieve their mutual ordering'.[2] I do not altogether accept this contrast between 'objective reality' on one side and mere 'thoughts' on the other; nor do I agree with the further assumption that, in primitive societies, the second kind of order appears exclusively in the guise of myth and religion. But this is not the main point, which is, rather, that the two kinds of 'order' exist side by side. As will be remembered, we in fact made this coexistence a basic condition of our whole search for the 'ordered arrangement' of societies; for we posited that the behaviour from which it is abstracted must be conceived, by the actors, as behaviour following from rights and obligations, that is, must have the implication of norms believed-in (or 'orders thought-of').

Now this means that behaviour guided, in some fashion, by the actors' notions on desirable or normal conduct will also yield, upon structural analysis, given constancies of conduct, and hence empirical-statistical norms. But the two are clearly of an entirely different logical order. In one case we have roles and relationships which flow from rules; in the other, the rules themselves. In the first, we deal with variable actions from which we abstract a positional picture, with its 'degrees of freedom'; in the second, we record assertions, beliefs and instructions on how to act—a *pragmatic design*, from which we abstract nothing and in regard to which we can only state the degree to which it is impressed, sanctioned, and obeyed. If the observed behaviour and the rules about it fully tally, we shall be able to say that the structure abstracted conforms to the structure envisaged and believed-in. Often, there will be no such complete coincidence. In which event the statistical norm will cover behaviour which, compared with the pragmatic design, evidences circumventions or modifications of it or, conceivably, individual 'choices and

---

[1] *Social Organization of the Western Pueblos*, p. 5.
[2] Op. cit. p. 548.

decisions' in the full sense of the word. However much or little the asserted rules and beliefs coincide with the norms demonstrated by structural analysis, the two must be kept separate; not to do so would be to reify an analytical construct.

This brings me to the second misunderstanding which, I suggested, is apt to obscure discussions of social structure. But before turning to this new topic I want to go back to a point raised a little earlier, when we considered it possible that the sequence of individual options might result in some total shift or realignment. This eventuality may well have radical consequences; for it implies nothing less than the possibility that all our calculations of 'workable constancy' or stability may be at fault.

4

Stability and its persuasive near-synonym, a stable equilibrium, are difficult concepts to handle. They imply at least three different though related operational criteria. First, we speak of social stability or equilibrium when we discover a far-reaching regularity and repetitiveness in social phenomena, that is, when some definable state of affairs can be said by and large to reproduce itself; these conditions are satisfied in all 'stationary states'. Secondly, we speak of stability or equilibrium when a regular state of affairs, on being upset by some identifiable 'disturbance', reasserts itself, either reverting to the *status quo* or reproducing itself in modified form. Thirdly, we speak of stability (though not perhaps of equilibrium) when we wish to indicate that particular social phenomena, institutions or relationships, last a long time or run their full course—that marriages do not end in divorce, families do not break up, or monarchies are not threatened by revolutions. In a sense this criterion is a corollary to the second, referring to the absence of disturbances altogether. But it implies an additional notion, that of some design inherent in the institution or relationship in accordance with which every instance of it (every marriage, family, or political regime) has a normal or optimum life expectancy; anything that falls short of this expectancy is then a sign of instability. To some extent, too, we may have our own preconceptions about this, and smuggle in our own value judgments.

There is a fourth criterion, though I doubt if it can often be applied with the requisite quantitative accuracy. If a set of interrelated institutions or relationships changes together progressively and approximately at the same rate, in the same or in complementary directions, so that the changes induce no upsets or disturbances, we may still speak of stability. For example, expanding kin groups may undergo progressive segmentation, the increase in the number of segments being paralleled by some workable internal reapportionment of rights and duties. Or families and kin groups will contract in effective size and in importance, while other, extraneous institutions (e.g. co-operatives, schools, political and welfare agencies), taking over the respective functions, will expand in the same proportion. Again, secular authority might steadily gain over religious authority, which is freely surrendered step by step. Or virilocal residence might gradually replace uxorilocal residence, the various concomitant conditions (land titles, group loyalties, facilities for upbringing of children) being adjusted correspondingly. Situations of this kind would exemplify the 'moving equilibrium' of economists and something in the nature of 'moving constancies' (Parsons) or a 'moving structure'.

Whichever way the three or four criteria may appear combined in practice, they inevitably involve a time scale. For it is clear that we need some time—some statistical 'run'—to be sure that the sequences of events are repetitive, that disturbances are offset, or that relationships and institutions run their full course or change at an even rate. And here it is not nonsensical to suggest that in anthropological observations the run may not be long enough for that. As Leach recently emphasized, our field studies are by and large of short duration; and if it is true of the social sciences in general that they deal with 'short statistical runs', too short to give results comparable with those of natural science, this must be doubly true of anthropology.[1]

The 'run' that should enable us to identify stability in social processes is clearly not uniform. The verification of repetitiveness, of restoration after disturbance, or of a 'full course' run by some institution, involve widely different time spans or scales. This assumption of a variety of time scales necessary to demon-

[1] Norbert Wiener, *Cybernetics*, p. 191.

strate stability is well known in economics. It closely corresponds to Samuelson's suggestion that equilibrium processes should be visualized as being 'of quite different speed', so that 'within each long run there is a shorter run, and within each shorter run there is a still shorter run, and so forth in an infinite regression'.[1] In practice, this means that some long-run stability (e.g. of a cyclical nature) is not identifiable on a shorter time scale; that a relatively short-run stability (e.g. a cumulative progression), is not identifiable on a still shorter time scale, etc. Our broad distinction between macro-time and micro-time obviously cannot cope with this picture of 'runs within runs'; nor is it necessary to make full allowance for it. Let me therefore modify our simple schema only a little. Using one which is still very simple, I shall include three possibilities, expressed in terms of the relative magnitudes of the micro- and macro-time scales: the schema would then indicate the time conditions that need to be satisfied if our judgments on stability are to be more than guesswork.

Relation between time scales	Processes visible on Mi-sc	Processes visible on Ma-sc
Ma-sc $>$ mi-sc	Sequences of events, positional movements, 'choices and decisions'	Repetitiveness, regularity, 'stationary states'
Ma-sc $\gg$ mi-sc		'Disturbances', cumulative changes
Ma-sc $\ggg$ mi-sc		Restoration of *status quo*, cycles, oscillations, continuous trends, 'moving equilibrium'

The absolute magnitudes of the periods involved need not worry us; in anthropology, they are in any event determined for

[1] P. A. Samuelson, *Foundations of Economic Analysis*, 1948, p. 330.

us, by the year or two we can spend in the field, by the ten or fifteen years before possible revisits, and by the few generations whose past is adequately recorded or less adequately remembered. What matters is the dependence of our inferences about stability or the opposite on suitable time spans; and since we cannot predict them nor be sure which phase we are actually facing, our inferences must remain hypothetical. Which raises the question, how far the respective hypotheses are useful or reasonable in the light of some general probability.

When making judgments on constancies, stability or equilibrium two considerations always enter. The first is a strictly empirical one, since 'it is simply a fact that . . . these constancies are often found to exist'.[1] The second is a heuristic one, the stipulated stability being a theoretical condition, a useful 'methodological fiction', required by the type of analysis we are after. It may in fact have the character of a postulate without which our particular investigation could not be carried out. Thus, if we are concerned (as in fact we are) with discovering the mutual determination of a plurality of elements, as in a 'system', we shall naturally assume, to begin with, that such a determination exists; in which case we must also assume the possibility of a complete state of this kind, a state wholly determined by the interrelation of all elements, and hence unchangeable while the elements are what they are. This is in essence Pareto's classical definition of social equilibrium as the 'real, normal state' of any system conceived to be so fully determined by the 'actions of its elements' that it can be made to vary only by extraneous 'artificial factors'.[2] The heuristic value of such assumptions or postulates needs no explaining; the use of the equilibrium model in economics proves it amply.

It is worth noting that, when we make these assumptions, in regard to societies or any other universe of discourse, it is not the equilibrium conditions *as such* which matter to us most or primarily. There is nothing inherently important about them. Purely objectively (and ignoring the viewpoint of welfare) human communities in a state of equilibrium are neither better nor worse, neither more nor less interesting than in any other

---

[1] Talcott Parsons, *The Social System*, p. 482.
[2] Pareto, *The Mind and Society*, §§ 2067, 2070.

state. The assumption of equilibrium is important only in a derived sense, as the logical consequence of that more fundamental assumption, that it makes sense to look for determinacy. If we believed in a social universe entirely characterized by the free will of all its elements, we should not need equilibrium assumptions; nor indeed could we use them in any profitable way.

Now if, in anthropology, there were any real doubts about our empirical evidence for constancies and forms of stability, we should be moving entirely in the realm of as-if constructions, however useful. And one anthropologist, at least, doubts even this usefulness. Thus Leach has recently castigated the English anthropologists for holding 'false assumptions' of this kind. In spite of the fact, or perhaps because of it, that the anthropologist studies only 'the population of a particular place at a particular point in time', he tends to present his data as though the societies described 'are as they are, now and for ever'. He is indeed guilty also of other shocking misdemeanours, though these I shall disregard (feeling guiltless myself). The gist of it is that anthropologists are simply prejudiced in favour of stability and equilibrium. If descriptions in this vein have any value it is only the odd one of meeting the tastes of the reader, to whom any other kind of analysis 'would certainly appear . . . incomplete'. Otherwise, a society in equilibrium is merely 'the anthropologist's hypothesis about "how the social system works" '—a 'model of social reality', no more.[1]

The answer to all this is, in a word, that the assumptions in question are neither false nor dragged in without reasons. Our hypotheses and as-if constructions are not fantasies but well grounded, both methodologically and empirically. For the empirical constancies do exist and are observable; nor presumably would anyone have conceived of equilibrium models, in economics or elswhere, if empirical observations had not suggested something like them in the first place. Let us admit this, however. The constancies which we, the anthropologists in the field, actually observe are of short range. We do see repetitions, regularities, the reproduction of roles and relationships, and the restoring of (small-scale) disturbed states—as in disputes,

[1] E. R. Leach, *Political Systems of Highland Burma*, pp. 6-8.

quarrels, unexpected fatalities, etc. But we also assume them to last longer than the period of observation. In other words, we anticipate the appropriate scale of macro-time on which our assumptions would really be proved. We surely have good grounds for doing so: they lie in the observable maintenance machineries; in past continuities, ascertainable with a fair degree of reliability; and, last but not least, in our general faith that a living society will not change its shape as soon as our backs are turned.

We do nowadays work in primitive societies so exposed to extraneous influences that they might literally change as soon as our backs are turned. But they would not change for that reason, which is the crux of our faith and the foundation of our whole science. No one would dream of stretching his faith so far as to believe that stationary states go on for ever and that any disturbance (unspecified) will be overcome by a return to the *status quo*. All that we could say or think of saying is that if stationary states, or 'structures', cease to be what they are, there must be a reason—which is as banal as it is fundamental; and that, if they are 'disturbed', a further state is possible or likely which will once more produce relative stability, in a new structure or the old one restored. To what extent or after what interval changing conditions will permit this re-emergence of constancies, and what they will look like, may be beyond even the scope of hypotheses. But if no workable constancies emerge, then there is no society for us to study and no structure to define; for the assumptions or postulates underlying our methods also prescribe the nature of the data that can be studied by them.

Finally, there remain three conditions which we cannot satisfy, given the short range of our observations. (i) We cannot judge whether the options and choices actually made (e.g. concerning occupations and careers, residence on marriage, reliance on paternal or maternal kin) represent some balance that will prove stationary in the long run, or an imbalance tending to produce cumulative effects and progressive trends. (ii) We cannot judge how far such trends are progressing at an even rate, in a 'moving equilibrium' or 'moving structure', or will be arrested at some point, in a structure so-and-so rearranged and stabilized. (iii) Nor can we judge whether such *de facto* options and choices as we have reason to regard as breaks in the pre-existing stability (e.g. the premature dissolution of families, the weakening of marriage rules, the growth of illegitimate power) are just that or form part of some self-compensating oscillation and pendulum swing, or again, of some progressive trend.

These are serious limitations; but they are of a technical, not of a logical, nature. Though we shall never have the 'long runs' of the natural scientist, whose time scale is attuned to 'eternity and ubiquity' (Wiener), we can make them much longer than they are now. The accumulation of descriptive data combined with re-studies will help; so will, to an even greater extent, continuous observations over really long periods, such as, I understand, Russian anthropologists are now carrying out. Until such evidence is available our judgments on stationary states, stability and instability, trends or oscillations, will remain working hypotheses, only partly verifiable. But this chance of long-range observations would be wasted unless there are relevant facts to observe. Which means that we must go on hypothesizing about stability and the rest if only to provide others with useful clues, that is, with assumptions to confirm or refute.

5

We turn to our next problem, the trap of *reification*. What I have said so far on this head, contrasting empirical norms with pragmatic designs, the abstraction of behavioural regularities with the rules imposing them, could be stated more simply. Once more borrowing from Lévi-Strauss, we could call social structure a 'statistical model';[1] for it has the same degree of reality (or non-reality) which we should ascribe to any purely statistical picture of a social situation. By contrast, there are the 'mechanical models' of societies, exemplified by their valid laws, marriage laws, for example, 'calling for actual groupings of the individuals according to clan and kin'. This contrast can be expressed more sharply. It is only the pragmatic design of societies, their body of rules backed by sanctions, which can be ascribed concrete efficacy and 'real' consequences, positive in

[1] In *Anthropology Today*, p. 528.

determining conduct, and negative in failing to prevent disobedience or non-conformity. The statistical model can have no such efficacy, positive or negative, and there can be no efforts to assail or circumvent it. The variations it exhibits can logically be represented only as 'degrees of freedom', perhaps as 'thresholds' (Lévi-Strauss) or as zones of indeterminacy, and hence as indices of the probability with which its constancies apply.

Yet this logical distinction is often ignored. We find descriptions of social structure in wholly 'realistic' terms, as when Firth calls it a 'reliable guide to action', which on occasion can be disregarded, or when other scholars talk about social structure 'maintaining itself', exercising 'pressure', or 'resisting' the impact of change. Radcliffe-Brown and Evans-Pritchard speak, somewhat picturesquely, of 'individuals passing through the social structure'. Clearly, an orderliness abstracted from behaviour cannot guide behaviour, resist change, or be 'passed through' by living people. It is instructions, asserted rules and beliefs which influence action, are disregarded, or upheld under conditions of change; and it is only of the offices, roles, tasks, and institutions established by such rules that we can say that people assume and discard them or 'pass through' in their lifetime.

These are not perhaps serious confusions; the reification they introduce is probably merely the result of a loose use of language. But precisely for this reason they suggest that we need another concept if we are to avoid the risk of inaccuracy. As I see it, this concept must cover two sets of facts: first, the normative assertions, beliefs, and instructions current in the society in so far as they bear on roles and relationships; and secondly, the institutionalized practices designed to produce and maintain the state of affairs in question. In other words, the new concept will have to be analogous to social structure in generality, but its counterpart in reference, the reference now being to the operativeness of society, that is, to its *codifications* and its *maintenance machinery* (see pp. 51ff.). Though I originally included in the latter only sanctioning (or 'control') mechanisms proper, it is logical to extend the meaning of maintenance also to recruitment principles, since they too 'maintain' and 'control'. They do so only as regards the obtaining distribution and arrangement of roles and relationships, being themselves subject to further, sanctioning, controls; but we may disregard this complication. The concept most adequately summarizing this operative counterpart to social structure is *organization* as developed by Firth. He speaks of organization in precisely this sense, as being 'complementary' to social structure and as representing, in brief, 'the working arrangements of society', whereby a group (so-and-so structured) 'is kept in being'.[1]

This complementary juxtaposition of structure and organization could be analysed and elaborated further. For example, we could relate organization, since it implies aim-directed activities operating as such, to what I have called the dimension of action (or *culture*); while social structure, resting as it does on the abstraction of the actor-to-actor linkages, belongs to the opposite dimension of relationships and groupings (or *society*).[2] And we might perhaps give to 'codification' a more autonomous status, regarding it as part of the idea and value system of societies. Firth, in another context, outlines much the same triadic division when he mentions three principal objectives of social enquiry—structure, organization, and values.[3]

There is no need to carry this argument further. Let me break off at this point and return once more to the question of the 'reality' of social structure. Though I adopted Lévi-Strauss's description of social structure as a 'model' I should make it clear that his use of the word has certain implications, concerning this question of reality, which do not agree with the views here expressed. For Lévi-Strauss 'social structure has nothing to do with empirical reality but with models built after it'; and these must be such that 'they make immediately intelligible all the observed facts'.[4] Nor is Lévi-Strauss alone in upholding the model character, in this sense, of social structure. Leach, very similarly, considers 'the structures which the anthropologist describes' to be nothing more real than 'models which exist only as logical constructions in his mind'. Again, analysis in terms of

[1] 'Social Organization and Social Change', *J.R.A.I.*, vol. 84, p. 10.
[2] See my *Foundations*, pp. 78 et seq.
[3] 'The Study of Values by Social Anthropologists', Marett Lecture, *Man*, 1953, 231, p. 2.
[4] In *Anthropology Today*, p. 525.

structure seems to deserve that name only if it improves upon reality; structural description 'provides us with an idealized model which states the "correct" status relations between groups . . . and . . . social persons'.[1]

Now I am not prepared to dismiss empirical reality so completely from the positional picture we call a social structure. Its statistical nature apart, it has some remoteness from 'real conditions'—the remoteness that goes with progressive abstraction and as-if assumptions. But these are still methods whereby we attempt to catch reality as best we can, not devices for reconstructing or idealizing it 'in our mind'. Undoubtedly, there is nothing to prevent one from thinking about social structure in the latter way. It simply seems to me arbitrary as well as unhelpful. To begin with, it makes it impossible for us to speak of studying or investigating social structure: for you do not study or investigate a model—you 'build' it, on the basis of empirical investigations, and you manipulate it, so that you may better understand the empirical phenomena. Furthermore, if we accept the proposition of these two scholars the question arises what to call the thing we study and wish to understand, that is, the thing the model is a model of. Lévi-Strauss's answer seems to be 'social relations'; at least, they are said to be 'the raw material out of which the models making up social structure are built'. But this is surely underrating both the coherence of social life and the competence of social analysis. In either case there are wider units or networks of units to be reckoned with than so-and-so many discrete and disjointed 'social relations'. If we are to have explanatory models, they have to account for these wider and widest units as well; and the appropriate word to describe this kind of 'raw material' surely is social structure.

But the crucial difference in our views, Lévi-Strauss's and Leach's on one side, and mine on the other, lies in this. For Lévi-Strauss and Leach, structure is an explanatory construct meant to provide the key to the observed facts of social existence, the principles or formulae accounting for its character, and hence the logic behind social reality. I consider social structure, of whatever degree of refinement, to be still the social reality itself, or an aspect of it, not the logic behind it; and I consider

[1] *Political Systems of Highland Burma*, pp. 5, 9.

structural analysis to be no more than a descriptive method, however sophisticated, not a piece of explanation. Indeed, I am not sure that social structure is rightly called a 'model', if by this term we mean more than the reduction of a multifarious slice of reality to a simpler, more consistent picture, simpler and more consistent because it represents only one way of looking at reality. Usually, the word 'model' implies more than this, namely, a 'picture' so constructed that it has logical necessity and explanatory power, so that verifiable deductions can be made from it.[1] I do not think that social structure satisfies this latter, more rigorous, condition.

Particular problems posed by social structure may indeed be explored with the help of models, constructed out of the facts we know or suspect and manipulated so that they demonstrate unperceived consequences or variables. Our mutual-steering mechanism, meant to account for conformity and deviance in role behaviour, is a case in point (see pp. 51f.). Another example is Leach's own treatment of a kinship terminology as explainable on the basis of a few propositions and their logical consequences.[2] Whenever economists (or for that matter anthropologists) use equilibrium processes as clues to critical interdependences, they once more operate with true models. Perhaps we should do more of this, as Firth suggests. But the description of a social structure is a task of a different order. When we define the positional picture of a society, in terms of command or any other criterion, we only abstract an order from empirical reality without reconstructing or idealizing it more than we can help, or turning it into a model. I do not deny, of course, that any such picture will still tax our ingenuity since we shall also want the key to it, the principles or the logic underlying it. That is, we shall want to show not only what the social system looks like but 'how it works'. And in order to do this we may well have to reconstruct and idealize it 'in our mind'. Since explanation always spills over into description, the concepts needed for the former being foreshadowed in the latter, we shall no doubt draw our positional picture so that it will facilitate grasping its 'logic'; which may be a further reason why the social structure as

[1] See R. B. Braithwaite, *Scientific Explanation*, pp. 90-1, 108.
[2] 'Jinghpaw kinship terminology', *J.R.A.I.*, vol. 75, 1949.

described is in some measure removed from reality. But it is so removed not because it already produces the idealizing, explanatory model, but because it represents that degree of abstraction from and ordering of empirical reality without which we could not begin to think about explanations.

VII

CONCLUSIONS: STRUCTURE AND FUNCTION

It is time to draw the threads together. The last steps in this enquiry into what social structure 'really means' have shown it to be a conceptual tool both more and less powerful than is often assumed. In the final analysis, its weaknesses seem greatly to outweigh its strength, the greatest weakness being its narrow compass and, consequently, the fragmentation it imposes on our universe of discourse. As I put it before, it seems impossible to speak of social structure in the singular. Analysis in terms of structure is incapable of presenting whole societies; nor, which means the same, can any society be said to exhibit an embracing, coherent structure as we understand the term. There are always cleavages, dissociations, enclaves, so that any description alleged to present a single structure will in fact present only a fragmentary or one-sided picture.

Quite recently Firth drew the same conclusion from a more general viewpoint. To quote from his Presidential Address: 'There is . . . no such isolable entity (as) *the* social structure'; '*the* social structure, viewed as something within the grasp of the ethnographer's account, is a myth'. And again: 'If we want to compare structural systems . . . it is only in a selective sectional way that this can be done'.[1] We can fill in the relevant details. As we discovered, it is impossible even to articulate the different 'sectors' of social structure (or the several social structures of a society) with one another; at least, it cannot be done within the same logical framework, using only one set of terms. Rather, we need at least three different terms—recruitment, interpersonal command, and relative command over resources and benefits. Only the second set of terms corresponds to the conventional criterion of social structure, relationships in

[1] *J.R.A.I.*, vol. 84, 1954, p. 5.

virtue of direct interaction; the first indicates only the mechanics (or 'organizational' factors) underlying the assumption of positions and relationships; and the third introduces an extraneous reference point, defining relationships indirectly. Finally, the two command criteria demonstrate little more than the distribution of power and authority, so that social structure coincides with power and authority structure.

Thus defined, the social structure (structure in the plural) seems to have little informative value. It does enable us to sum up and visualize complex situations in the form of schemata, diagrams, and formulae. But if this final summary were all that we aim at, I cannot imagine anyone being very interested in it or deriving much enlightenment from the mere setting-out of command positions in stationary states. The final summary is actually a little more interesting since we should also include in it, once more, the conditions of recruitment, references to the permanence or mobility of the command positions, and perhaps certain other 'lower level abstractions'. But what makes structural analysis really information, it seems to me, is not the final positional picture at all, but the steps that lead to it. Our gain lies in the application of the appropriate analytical methods, not in gathering together, schematically, the results. For it is in the course of this application that we achieve a penetrating insight into the working of society. Every step in the many abstractions and comparisons we have to make reveals crucial interdependences—between individuals in their roles, between the roles and the rest of society, and between groups built out of roles. Above all, in progressively discounting the particular features of social situations (which is the essence of abstraction), we prepare the way for the discovery of general characteristics and regularities, and hence of the lawfulness—such lawfulness as obtains—in the realm of social existence. One or two examples have in fact been quoted.

Thus, paradoxically speaking, we profit not from having defined a social structure, but from trying to define it, not from having made the study but from making it. This is not as odd or paradoxical as it may sound. In a different context Firth similarly, and convincingly, argues that the importance of a certain analytical procedure (here concerning the 'Study of

Values'), 'lies not in the conclusions but in the refinement of our ideas produced by their discussion'.[1]

I doubt if the professed students of social structure will agree with this diluted appreciation of their key method. For one thing, they would probably reject my thesis about social structure being always in the plural.[2] And for another, they could undoubtedly quote several studies presenting the end results of structural analysis, in the form of dissertations on 'the social structure' of various groups, which give accounts highly coherent, informative, and rich in content—all the things I said could not be done by this method. But my colleagues and I should be talking about different things. For I would claim that none of these studies is one of social structure in the rigorous sense in which I have employed the word. The truth is that this concept, in spite of the various ambitious definitions supporting it, is being used in a lax and highly unanalysed fashion. What the students of social structure really do is to describe, still in heavily qualitative terms, types of relationships and groups, their interconnections through activities and recruitment, the believed-in values and norms of the people, and the obtaining sanctioning mechanisms; nor do they exclude the psychological concomitants of relationships ('loyalties', 'sentiments', and other motivations). In no sense do these studies bear out the claim of the 'structuralist' school that they follow rigorous procedures and aim at high-level abstractions.[3]

My point, therefore, is that the rich content and informative character of these studies is due, not to a rigorous structural analysis carried to its logical end, but to the fact that the studies fall short of this goal. They exemplify the 'structural point of view' (Radcliffe-Brown), and no more. They present all the steps in the analysis, all the intermediate stages, without applying the final degrees of abstraction. It follows from what I have said before that I do not regard this altogether as a failure.

[1] *Man*, 1953, 231, p. 2.
[2] Cf. Meyer Fortes: The concept of social structure 'draws attention to the interconnection and interdependence, *within a single system*, of all the different classes of social relations found within a given society'. (The italics are mine; see *American Anthropologist*, vol. 55, 1953, p. 22.)
[3] See E. E. Evans-Pritchard, *Social Anthropology*, 1951, p. 95.

This brings me back to the question raised at the very beginning of this enquiry, concerning the usefulness of a broad as against a strict definition of social structure. Has it now been settled, in the former sense, by the last remarks? It would seem so. Though it is unrealistic to talk about *a* social structure in the strict sense of the word, it is obviously as unrealistic to cease talking about structure in a broad sense, and so to deny to societies *structuring* of some form, degree or complexity. Indeed, the assumption of a structureless society or group is a contradiction in terms, or very nearly so. If we identify a human collectivity as a society or as a sub-group within a society, we do so precisely because it exhibits roles more or less definitely allocated, definable relationships and their 'bounded areas', and all the other features exemplifying the ordered and relatively constant arrangement of units. There are no true exceptions. Groups in states of disintegration or 'anomie', leaderless crowds, amorphous 'masses' and the like may indeed be said to lack structure (or structuring) altogether: but these are all human aggregates on the borders of social existence as we must understand it. It would seem to follow that the looser our definition of structure, the more adequately will it represent the actual subject matter of our studies.

I am not sure that this argument is as convincing as it sounds. If it is true, as I have suggested, that our knowledge is advanced by the procedures entailed in structural analysis, then the rigorous, strict conception of structure must have its value, if only the heuristic one of setting the aim high enough. With a broader and looser conception our insight into the working of society might not be as full and precise. And if the studies of social structure already available are informative and relevant, they will be more informative still, as well as more precise, if the analysis is given a stricter direction.

Moreover, in one respect the strict definition of social structure cannot be modified, and structural analysis must not fall short of the final level of abstraction. This is true of investigations implying comparisons and aiming at generalizations based on a wide range of instances. Structural analysis is clearly moving in this direction. Anthropologists are more and more concerned with tracing and explaining the appearance of identical structures in societies otherwise widely different (that is, differing in material conditions, in the 'content' and aims of customary behaviour, in brief, in 'culture'); think of Murdock's book or of Fortes's essay on 'The Structure of Unilineal Descent Groups'. A similar problem is posed by the persistence of social structure in 'continuing societies', apparently unaffected by 'big changes in everyday habit, in ritual customs and belief, and even in major economic and social goals'.[1] I need not repeat that the comparability of the data depends on a high degree of abstraction and ultimately on our ability to handle mere positional schemata. I would only point out that these schemata are basically the ones here developed; these wide comparisons all operate, if only tacitly, with the criteria to which our discussion has led us. For mostly the studies of invariant or persisting social structures are concerned with kinship systems and the principles of ordering kin—through lineages, unilateral or bilateral descent, and so forth. That is, they reduce the comparison of societies to a comparison of recruitment principles and their consequences. And where the relationships between people so recruited to roles and positions are further explored, this is done in terms of jural relations, in terms of Radcliffe-Brown's dual principle of *jus in rem* and *jus in personam*, which is only a transliteration of our two criteria of command.

One final point needs clarifying. There is one lack of 'information' in structural analysis which many students of social structure will not only admit but defend—all information bearing on the satisfaction of human needs, on biological necessity or the utility of human actions and institutions, that is, on purpose or 'function' in general. The exclusion of these viewpoints as extraneous to structural analysis is upheld with varying emphasis. But some exclusion there is; and it can of course be defended, on the grounds of the basic rule of scientific method, that scientific enquiry must proceed by way of *isolating* its problem area.[2] Scholars like Fortes do not disregard the heuristic character of this isolation; they claim no autonomy or completeness for the structural analysis of society. If 'social

[1] M. Fortes, op. cit. *American Anthropologist*, 1953, vol. 55, p. 23.
[2] See H. Levy, *The Universe of Science*, rev. ed., 1947, p. 4.

structure' must be separated from other ways of approach to the problems of human and social existence, this is only a separation of different 'frames of reference', all of which are ultimately justifiable and necessary.[1] Even so, there are indications that the 'structuralist' judges his own frame of reference to be not only heuristically useful and promising, but to be more useful and promising, and indeed more important, than the other frame of reference, resting on the concepts of utility, purpose, or 'function'.

All I wish to say on this point is that I cannot accept this judgment, and that I feel it is not enough merely to acknowledge the two ways of analysing social existence. As I see it, social existence belongs to a universe of discourse governed by the concepts of purpose and utility; the approach through structure cannot but be subordinated to them. This can be expressed more simply (if a little 'realistically'): social structures 'have jobs to do ... hence some structures will be more efficient for certain purposes and less so for others'.[2] The 'jobs' and 'purposes' are easy to define—making a living, satisfying whatever needs or desires human organisms are possessed of in given conditions. No amount of heuristic isolation can obscure the fact that the data of social structure have a bearing on the 'jobs' societies must do and on the purposes that require efficient handling. Nor must that bearing be pushed out of sight until we are ready to plan the ultimate reconciliation of the diverse 'frames of reference'. Rather, it must be allowed for in our very method of approach. Which means that there must be some articulation between the criteria of structural analysis and the concepts of purpose and utility.

I have allowed for this articulation. For in employing the criteria of command over persons and benefits I have introduced concepts connoting, if only implicitly, purpose and utility, since command always means command for some purpose. Earlier on, I justified this step by saying that these criteria help to retain a degree of relevance in structural analysis. I would now say that they help to retain, or provide, the necessary link-

[1] See 'The Structure of Unilineal Descent Groups', p. 21; *Social Anthropology at Cambridge since 1900*, pp. 38-41.
[2] Fred Eggan, *Social Organization of the Western Pueblos*, pp. 7, 297.

age between the theory of social structure and the social universe of purpose. You may call this an insurance against a heuristic isolation which can be driven too far, or a reminder that we live in societies where there are jobs to be done.